Let Mt. Zion
REJOICE!

Let Mt. Zion
REJOICE!

Music in the African
American Church

JAMES ABBINGTON

JUDSON PRESS
VALLEY FORGE

Let Mt. Zion Rejoice! Music in the African American Church
© 2001 by Judson Press, Valley Forge, PA 19482-0851
All rights reserved.

Library of Congress Cataloging-in-Publication Data

Abbington, James.
    Let Mt. Zion rejoice! : music in the African American church / James Abbington.
    p. cm.
    Includes bibliographical references.
    ISBN 0-8170-1399-7 (pbk. : alk. paper)
    1. Church music—United States—21st Century. 2. African Americans—Music—History and criticism. 3. African Americans—Religion. 4. African American churches. I. Title: Let Mt. Zion rejoice! II. Title.

ML3111 .A23 2001
264'.2'08996073—dc21   2001022996

Printed in the U.S.A.

07 06 05 04 03 02 01

10 9 8 7 6 5 4 3 2 1

With deep gratitude
and eternal love
to
Momma and Daddy

CONTENTS

ACKNOWLEDGMENTS

It is a sincere pleasure to acknowledge the obligations that I have incurred during the writing of this book:

Dr. J. Alfred Smith Sr., for publishing my first article in the Baptist Progress in 1988

Dr. Genna Rae McNeil for proofreading and editorial suggestions for chapters 7, 8, and 9

My cousin, Dr. Clarressa Morton, for proofreading, editorial suggestions, and initial formatting

Dr. Archie Logan, executive secretary for the General Baptist State Convention of North Carolina, for his support in publishing my essays "Psalms, Hymns, and Spiritual Songs"

Dr. Talbert O. Shaw, president, and Dr. Ernest L. Pickens, executive vice president, of Shaw University for the encouragement and support they offered while I was completing this project

I am eternally grateful to Dr. Nathaniel Tyler-Lloyd, senior pastor, and the Workshop Choir of the Trinity Baptist Church for their love, prayers, and continuous support.

ACKNOWLEDGMENTS

I am most indebted to William B. McClain for his guidance, encouragement, and confidence in my work throughout the course of this project.

I am grateful to my God-brother and friend, Dr. Carlyle Fielding Stewart III, for his intellectual and highly disciplined model and example.

PRELUDE

Three things characterized this religion of the slave—the Preacher, the Music, and the Frenzy.[1]

In the Black Church good preaching and good singing are almost invariably the minimum conditions of a successful ministry. Both activities trace their roots back to Africa where music and religion and life itself were all one holistic enterprise. [2]

A common dictum in Black church circles is, "you can't organize Black folks for anything without music." [3]

The African American church is the most important institution in the African American community. Its influence is so far-reaching that some scholars say the African American church *is* the African American community. The black church is the only black institution that has been continually shaped and developed by African Americans. [4]

W. E. B. Du Bois and C. Eric Lincoln have defined two of the black church's most essential components: the heartbeat, or preaching, and the bloodline, or singing. The importance of music as a tool for organizing African Americans is underscored in Wyatt Tee Walker's comment. But there is a scarcity of books, journals, and articles that deal specifically with music and worship in the African American church. One had to rely heavily on the general writings of such scholars as Du Bois, John W. Work III, Miles Mark Fisher, Benjamin E. Mays, E. Franklin Frazier, Carter G. Woodson, Bishop

PRELUDE

Daniel Payne, Wesley Gaines, Benjamin Brawley, Albert Raboteau, Howard Thurman, Eileen Southern, James H. Cone, Gayraud Wilmore, and a few others. These scholars in general, however, do not speak of music and worship specifically. Instead researchers and students of African American church music had to piece together accounts of church musicians, broad statements about music in worship, and the accounts of pastors and church musicians that speak to our history. These accounts tell of such pioneers as Charles Albert Tindley, Mahalia Jackson, Thomas A. Dorsey, Dr. A. M. Townsend and Willa (Mrs. A. M.) Townsend, Lucie E. Campbell, E. W. D. Isaac, Roberta Martin, William Herbert Brewster Sr., Edward Boatner, Kenneth Morris, and Doris Akers, to name the most popular.

Since the 1970s some significant and groundbreaking works have been published. The Liturgical Conference of the United States Catholic Conference, Inc., contributed *This Far by Faith* (1974). George Robinson Ricks wrote of *Some Aspects of the Religious Music of the United States Negro* (1977), which was followed by *Somebody's Calling My Name* by Wyatt Tee Walker (1979). J. Wendell Mapson Jr. provided two studies, *The Ministry of Music in the Black Church* (1984) and *Strange Fire* (1996, from lectures given in 1995–1996).

In almost every year of the 1990s, more material became available. In 1990 William B. McClain's *Come Sunday*, Jon Michael Spencer's *Protest and Praise*, and *Plenty Good Room*, published by the Secretariat for the Liturgy and Secretariat for Black Catholics National Conference of Catholic Bishops, went into print. Next came Spencer's *Black Hymnody (*1992), Melva Wilson Costen's *African American Christian Worship* (1993), and Walter F. Pitts's *Old Ship of Zion* (1993).

Among the most recent works are *Saints in Exile* (1996) by Cheryl J. Sanders, *Praising in Black and White* (1996) by Brenda Eatman Aghahowa, and *African American Worship* (1998) by Frederick Hilborn Talbot.

Over the past two decades John Lovell Jr., Bernice Johnson Reagon, Horace Clarence Boyer, Michael W. Harris, Cheryl Kirk-

Duggan, Arthur C. Jones, Irene V. Jackson-Brown, Portia Maultsby, Mellonee V. Burnim, Lawrence W. Levine, and Pearl Williams Jones have provided the most reliable and unparalleled scholarship about Negro spirituals and gospel music in their books and articles.

My intent is to concentrate on selected topics and areas in African American church music that have been neglected or rarely discussed in print. Many of these topics, among them musicians' qualifications, worship planning, and a proposal for observance of an African American Christian Year, have not been dealt with.

The title of this book was inspired by J. B. Herbert's anthem "Let Mt. Zion Rejoice," which is a setting of Psalm 48. It is probably the most popular and most sung anthem of the African American church. Herbert's setting includes the following verses (KJV):

> Great is the LORD, and greatly to be praised in the city of our God, in the mountain of his holiness (v. 1)
> Beautiful for situation, the joy of the whole earth, is mount Zion (v. 2)
> We have thought of thy lovingkindness, O God, in the midst of thy temple (v. 9)
> According to thy name, O God, so is thy praise unto the ends of the earth: thy right hand is full of righteousness (v. 10)
> Let mount Zion rejoice, let the daughters of Judah be glad (v. 11)
> Walk about Zion, and go round about her: tell the towers thereof (v. 12)
> Mark ye well her bulwarks, consider her palaces; that ye may tell it to the generation following (v. 13)
> For this God is our God for ever and ever; he will be our guide even unto death (v. 14)

Like Psalm 46, a hymn of Zion, Psalm 48:2-3 focuses on the motifs of the divine mountain and the defeat of the nations gathered against Israel. Another motif of Zion, the pilgrimage to the sanctuary, is presented in verses 9-13. The context of the psalm is military: defense of the city against the attack. The beauty of the city, the conviction that the city is "the joy of all the earth," is intimately related to its impregnability. For the practical Israelite, a beautiful city is a strong city; in their world the purpose of a city is defense.[5] This principle is one that Thomas Peter Wahl further exegetes:

> In an exhortation that surely relates to a ritual procession, the congregation is called to walk around the city inspecting its fortifications "that you may tell the next generation that such is our God" (v. 14). Remarkably, it is through the defenses of the city that God is known! So the poem returns to where it began, not with self-satisfaction over the security of the city, but with the greatness of Yahweh. . . . The Christian of today can pray the psalm in rejoicing at the historical Jerusalem. However flawed that ancient city may have been, it is through Zion that in fact we have to come to know our God.[6]

As Christians, we are no longer praying for the Jerusalem of old, but we may well pray the psalm in terms of those things in our lives that best correspond and relate to the Jerusalem of the psalm. The Christian exultation in the Zion of the church or of one's religious community, like that of the ancient Israelites, dare not be unconditional. Absolute praise or absolute adherence to any but God is idolatry.[7] The psalm finally is the praise not of Zion but of God who protects Zion. It begins and ends with God: "Great is the LORD, and greatly to be praised."

The African American church has been and is the Mt. Zion of our community--the invincible city of God. Lincoln said that "in the early black church the first emphasis was on getting to know God more intimately, and getting used to the idea that black people were not 'cursed of God,' nor condemned by God to be 'hewers of wood and drawers of water' for white people who called themselves 'master.' The church brought the comfort and security of God's love and redemption into the hopelessness of abject dereliction."[8] The black response—the prayer and the preaching, the singing, the moaning, the shouting or, as Du Bois put it, the frenzy—kept the human spirit alive and the presence of God an assured consolation.

The African American church has not been without its

challenges, struggles, faults, and failures. However, it remains the only institution that African Americans have founded, owned, operated, and continue to develop. Wahl, writing about the Christian church in general, succinctly summarizes my feelings about the African American church: "Despite all the failure of compassion that I have known in the Church—and which I have myself committed in the Church's name—all the blindness to issues of justice, despite all the arrogance, greed, and exploitation, still it is in this same Church that I have been challenged by the gospel, that I have seen something of the living Christ in the lives and work and wisdom of men and women who have been touched by that gospel. It is in this Church that I have known pardon and love."[9]

Let Mt. Zion Rejoice! is a practical resource for pastors, music directors, musicians, church staffs, congregational worship committees, theologians, seminarians, teachers and students of church music, choir members, and anyone involved in music and worship in the African American church. It is intended for those who take the ministry of music seriously and who commit themselves regularly to the study, preparation, and presentation of musical excellence in worship.

The first chapter is an analysis of the current state of music in the African American church and a call to action for the challenges that must be faced. Chapter 2 discusses the categories of musicians serving in churches today. Chapter 3 addresses fundamentals for church musicians, while chapter 4 looks at the essential relationship between pastors and musicians. Chapter 5 critically examines the choirs in African American churches.

In chapter 6 I shall focus on the importance of planning worship, and I will suggest ways of improving the experience. In chapters 7, 8, and 9 I look at three genres of music in the African American church: hymns, anthems, and congregational spirituals. Finally, in chapter 10 I give recommendations on integrating the Christian Year into our worship services, with an emphasis on using African American music and religious traditions to strengthen our Christocentric focus and mission.

Material in these chapters has been selected from various

lectures, workshops, and frequently asked questions about music in the African American church. Hardly a week goes by that I don't receive a telephone call, e-mail, fax, or flyer from pastors, musicians, music committee members, deacons, trustees, and search committees looking for musicians. It seems unreal that churches with active membership of more than fifteen hundred individuals--ready, willing, eager, and capable of compensating a musician--can't find a worthy candidate. This problem is not limited to African American churches but applies in Christian churches all over the United States. Churches that have musicians or that are fortunate to find musicians frequently complain that the musician lacks adequate preparation, commitment, and knowledge about music and worship in the church.

It is my sincere hope that this book will provide information, inspiration, challenge, and edification for the ministry of music in the African American church and that its suggestions can be implemented in local churches. Information and education without application waste and misuse knowledge.

Let Mt. Zion rejoice!

CHAPTER ONE

THE CURRENT STATE OF MUSIC IN THE AFRICAN AMERICAN CHURCH

T HERE WAS A TIME IN MANY AFRICAN AMERICAN CHURCHES
when musicians were plentiful. There were even waiting lists
at some churches. Many mainline churches (Baptist,
Methodist, and Presbyterian) were fortunate to have local
public-school or college music teachers as organists and
choir directors. There were students taking piano lessons privately
and even scholarships for students to further their musical education beyond secondary school. Commitment and dedication were
almost automatically coupled with skill and training. Musicians
worked for little or nothing in the church and rarely took a Sunday
off except for an annual two-week vacation.

But times have changed. What has happened? What has caused
the current shortage of musicians, and why are so many churches
unhappy with their musicians?

Until the mid-1970s, church music programs seemed to be
flourishing and productive for that time. Choir stands were full.
Organ benches were occupied by trained musicians, the hymnal
was being used extensively, and the European American musical
culture that greatly influenced the black church had little or no
tolerance for the emerging gospel music of James Cleveland,
Andrae Crouch, and Edwin Hawkins, and only some arranged spirituals sung as anthems set the standards. Musicians were trained and
could be depended upon to render the services for which they had
been hired. However, few churches were offering music instruction
and preparing the next generation of young people for church

1

music. Nor were they willing to accept, teach, and adapt to the rise of gospel music.

Changes in the national culture have had a prodigious influence on the music and worship in the African American church in the past forty years. The 1960s saw the civil rights movement, black nationalism, Elijah Muhammad and the Nation of Islam's nationalist critique of Christianity as the white man's religion, the black power movement, James H. Cone's articulation of black theology, and the commercialization and industrialization of gospel music with the recording of Hawkins's "Oh Happy Day." In the 1970s Molefi Asante developed the theme of Afrocentricity. Through the 1980s were felt the rushing mighty winds of neo-Pentecostalism, and free-spirit, charismatic, and evangelical independent churches attracted many mainline church members.

"During the 1960s," asserts Robert M. Franklin, "dramatic changes began to unfold in the congregational culture of black churches. As black people embraced their African identities, they began to incorporate African religious practices into their liturgies. Some observers referred to this phenomenon as the re-Africanization of black Christianity. I characterize this process of retrieving African practices with the metaphor of being baptized in the Nile River, a redemptive process of reclaiming one's spiritual origins. Consequently, the energy of revival-style, folk religion began to emerge in black churches with conventional liturgical practices."[1]

As this style emerged many churches abandoned Euro-American anthems, hymns, pipe organs, traditional choir robes, and familiar liturgies, replacing them with gospel music, Hammond organs, drums, tambourines, electric guitars, hand clapping, rocking, and swaying--forms that had once been associated with the sanctified holiness church, or the holy rollers.

Cheryl J. Sanders says, "The Sanctified Church is an African American Christian reform movement that seeks to bring its standards of worship, personal morality, and social concern into conformity with a biblical hermeneutic of holiness and spiritual

empowerment."[2] C. Eric Lincoln and Lawrence Mamiya have
noted that

> A confusion as to the distinction between Holiness and
> Pentecostal groups persists to the present time, and is exacer-
> bated by the fact that in actual practice the lines distinguishing
> the two groups have been substantially blurred. So far as some
> believers are concerned there is no distinction, for these groups
> embrace both the requirements of conversion and of holiness
> or sanctification as prerequisite for salvation as well as the
> "third work of grace" called the baptism in the Holy Ghost,
> which is manifested in glossolalia or "speaking in tongues."[3]

Wyatt Tee Walker writes that "in the recent past, gospel music was
frequently taboo and Spirituals seldom used unless rendered as
anthems. This transparent snobbery toward Black sacred music,
whether intentional or not, is a form of self-rejection."[4]

With the rise of gospel music and neo-Pentecostal worship services, the need for trained musicians diminished; the ability to read
music and play hymns were no longer prerequisites for a church
musician in most churches.[5] As long as a musician could play by
ear, teach parts by rote from an album, and sing well, he or she
had the job.

Public-school education has reached a record low. The critical
issues of funding, class size, and standardized testing, all of which
affect secondary education, have impacted African American students. Many music programs have been discontinued or drastically
reduced because of funding cuts, and the effects of these reductions
have been felt severely in predominately African American public
schools. Therefore African American young people coming out of
high school are less likely to have been exposed to any music education. One rarely finds young people studying voice or instruments privately. If they sing in the school choirs or play in the band,
much of the learning is done by rote, repetition, and ear. The
fundamentals of music, sight singing and ear training, are not
offered in most high-school music programs. Many students who

are interested in private study find it difficult to pay for lessons or to find teachers who are sensitive to their individual gifts, talents, and learning styles.

Over the past few years the African American church has lost musicians through death, retirement, relocation, career changes, and economics. Countless numbers of these musicians, many of them in the prime of their careers, have not been replaced by equally competent musicians. Churches have had to take whomever they could get, and as a result, the level of the congregation's music has been suddenly redefined by the limitations and ability of the musician.

Adequate Salaries for Musicians

One of the most critical issues is the question of remuneration. Many musicians complain that salaries are not adequate for the amount of work that is required (see chap. 2). It is appropriate that we revisit the Levites, members of one of the twelve tribes and the appointed leaders of Old Testament worship. They were recognized as performing an important and sacred function in Israelite worship. They had to meet strict requirements and qualifications, because they were in the service of God. They were recognized and paid for their services (see Numbers 18:21; 2 Chronicles 31:2-10; Nehemiah 12:47; 13:5,10-11). Homes were to be provided for them (see Ezra 2:70; Nehemiah 7:73; 12:28-29,39).

There are those who say that paying musicians was under the law and that musicians should give their services to the church. But I don't recall that law being repealed under grace, and Walker appealed to a New Testament principle when he stated, "If the servant-is-worthy-of-his-hire principle is applicable to clergy, it must also be applicable to musicians. If it is inappropriate for a church to hire a jack-leg preacher, it is just as inappropriate to have a jack-leg musician."[6]

Many churches have not made music and worship priorities in their budgets. In his book *Somebody's Calling My Name*, Dr. Walker makes this concise observation:

> Good musicians cost money. The effective development of a
> musical program . . . will not proceed with a church policy
> alone. It must have the parallel budget commitment. Church
> musicians generally have received short shrift for any number
> of reasons too varied to list here. The primary reason is low-
> budget priority. It will become the responsibility of the church
> leadership to see to it that the companion budget commit-
> ment is made attendant to the policy commitment.[7]

Some churches expect musicians to make bricks without straw. But
other churches provide plenty of straw and workers to assist and still
don't get bricks. A musician's compensation should be commensu-
rate with his or her training, duties, and responsibilities.

Still other churches pay musicians well to get them to accept a
position, but this practice leaves no room for musical growth and
development. Therefore the musician doesn't feel obligated to learn
to read music, play hymns or anthems, or enroll in continuing education opportunities, because he or she already makes a weekly
salary between $500 and $750, or an annual salary of $25,000 to
$40,000. This is a constant challenge in churches that enter into
financial agreements with musicians and later establish criteria,
duties, and responsibilities.

One critical factor must be considered when establishing a
music budget for the church. The musicians' salaries are not the
entire music budget. Churches tend to consider salaries as the total
music budget. While salaries are a great percentage of the budget,
other essential items must be taken into consideration: sheet music,
supplies, musical instruments, equipment, robes and their regular
maintenance, professional growth and development for the music
staff, workshops, seminars and conferences, and concerts.

In "Music in the Churches of Black Americans: A Critical
Statement," the late Wendell P. Whalum stated:

> There is probably no element of black-church life more per-
> plexing and pathetic than its music and what we have let hap-
> pen to it. Not only have a conglomerate of styles and functions
> crept into our church music, but there seems to be little

knowledge of the "why music in worship" concept in the minds of those whose responsibility it is to govern the church and its music. The pathetic thing is that some of the music most often enjoyed by worshippers offers little to them by way of Christian education or kingdom building, and that the effects of its performance last only a few minutes after its "embers" fade away.

As I see it, both the clergy and the musicians are to be blamed for what has occurred and, logically, it is their responsibility to correct it. Some of the blame, too, must be shared by those of us who, in addition to being practicing church musicians, have little by little abdicated our responsibility for instructing those who have not had good solid training, but who, for various reasons, assume the task of musical leadership. We are therefore guilty of standing by, through the years, watching music in the black church deteriorate to a large degree, and even decay to some extent.[8]

Some churches and musicians have not abdicated their responsibility of training and preparing musicians for musical leadership. I know of outstanding programs and instruction in churches in Baltimore, Philadelphia, New York, Atlanta, Chicago, and Oakland, California, and of course there are others.

Adequate Instruments and Facilities

In addition to the lack of musicians to fill many positions across the country, some churches are either unwilling or unable to provide adequate musical instruments and facilities. There are churches where the pianos are not regularly tuned, the organs have not been serviced or repaired, and the sound systems are the archenemy of sound production. Improper installation and placement of organ consoles and speakers, the placement of other instruments (e.g., pianos, drums, electric guitars, synthesizers, amplifiers), and an overabundance of carpet in choir lofts can create acoustical nightmares. And these are just some of the most common and major problems in most churches. These factors reduce the effectiveness of music and worship. Speakers and drum sets that are improperly placed can be annoying and distracting during a worship service.

A properly designed, installed, and operated sound system can make services more worshipful, meaningful, and audible. It can improve the intelligibility of speech and the musical renditions, the quality of sound for tapes and broadcast ministries, the audio ambience as it affects the spiritual environment, and the ability of members who have some loss in their hearing to take part in the worship service.[9]

An improperly designed, installed, and operated sound system can create problems in each of these areas. And if no one on staff understands how to correct these problems as they are recognized, the problems combine to become greater than their individual parts. Correcting the situation then becomes an overwhelming task and may become nothing more than a topic of lively debate for years. It won't be resolved until someone is tired enough of the situation to deal with it.

But resolving an existing problem or setting out on the right path takes education. Quality audio equipment costs a considerable amount of money, and it is difficult to convince members of a sound committee about the realities of the professional audio world when poorly educated people offer poor advice. They become confused about who's right.[10] It becomes especially difficult when the person responsible for presenting these ideas to the decision makers is not equipped with the words to express the need and the ultimate benefit of a great system to the staff and the congregation.

Finally, contemporary worship services, while they are popular and attractive to new seekers, are often seen as performance exercises and religious entertainment. The lights-camera-action dramas, complete with hip-hop and reggae dancing, sequined costumes, warm-up suits, and tennis shoes, is appealing to megachurches and in television evangelism. As Walker observed, "The tremendous and deleterious impact of television, the Hollywood syndrome and the dilution of our religious art-form by pop-artists and their imitations have congealed the central purpose for which we gather on the Lord's Day."[11]

Praise and worship teams in many of the traditional, mainline churches often meet with some of the new-old challenges of congregational participation. There are people who don't come to church to praise and worship God. Instead they come to be spectators of worship. All the singing, prompting, clapping, and rhythmical and melodically intense repertoire won't lift the conservative, traditional worshiper in most mainline churches. Praise and worship teams that have a clearly defined mission and function in worship and that accept their role as worship leaders and not "mini-Supremes" or "pseudo-Temptations," entertainers, or praise-seekers, are most effective in churches that have been properly conditioned and orientated into the meaning and concept of praise and worship. Seminars, books, and videos have been produced to assist the effectiveness of praise and worship teams.

As we work to improve the quality of our musicians, our facilities, and our worship, so Mt. Zion will rejoice.

CHAPTER TWO

MUSICIANS IN THE CHURCH

I N *20 HOT POTATOES CHRISTIANS ARE AFRAID TO TOUCH,* Tony Campolo discusses such issues as AIDS, women in ministry, wealth, euthanasia, and remarriage of divorced persons. The one hot potato that Campolo missed is what we do about the problems with the music and musicians in our church. In many churches even the pastor is afraid or reluctant to touch this hot potato. However, the issue is critical and should be dealt with in a Christian and professional manner. An honest, accurate assessment of the various categories of musicians serving in African American churches is essential to evaluation of the music and worship life of the church.

Categories of Musicians

Before I begin any discussion of the types of "problem musicians" serving in most African American churches today, I must commend and congratulate what I consider to be some of the finest models of church musicians to be found anywhere in this country. They are well trained, dedicated, loyal, competent, and above all, Christian! Their work has been unswervingly consistent. Their music and worship experiences are rich and diverse, well planned and well prepared, enthusiastically presented and Spirit-filled. They are committed to fruitful partnership and consistent dialogue with their pastors. They can be found in churches small and large, urban and rural, north, east, south, and west, Baptist, Methodist, Presbyterian, and all those denominations in between.

Unfortunately, in too many of our churches, the musicians and ministers of music are less than one would hope for to lead the congregation in worship. In 1985 Wendell P. Whalum identified five categories of problematic music personnel who were serving in many churches.

Talented but untrained musicians. These musicians often cannot read music, have no knowledge of choir organization or choral directing, and have no awareness of the historical importance of the hymns, liturgy, or religious service.
Untrained and untalented but willing musicians. This group, larger in number than one would suspect, is made up of people who have had one or two years of piano study and are willing to accept leadership because no one in the church will or can assume responsibility for the music.
Musicians with basic music training who accept church duties without understanding what the program should be about and how it should be conducted. The result is that much of what is offered is out of focus with the needs and understanding of the congregation.
Musicians with good training and previous exposure to excellent music who ignore the level of the congregation. Instead of educating the congregation, these musicians operate on a plane too sophisticated for the congregation. These musicians will frequently impose oratorios, cantatas, and pageants on people not yet educated in hymns and anthems and who are therefore not ready for extended works.
Musicians with excellent training who take an attitude of superiority and make no attempt to lift the level of musical awareness. This kind of musician is usually identified as the organist-director and will officiate only at Sunday morning services or at the funerals and weddings of prominent citizens in the community.[1]

Since that time, at least three new "problem" categories of music personnel can be found in our churches. One is the *artist in residence.* This person often has received national or international acclaim and has recorded CDs with one or two popular songs. The artist in residence appears for a limited number of rehearsals and the

Sunday morning worship services. He or she may perform only two or three Sundays a month, thus leaving the other Sundays to the youth and children or another musician. The artist is featured significantly in the worship services and usually leads the worship service, which includes leading praise and worship, singing the major solos, and perhaps playing the piano, organ, or electronic keyboards. In most cases the artist is unavailable to assume the day-to-day duties and responsibilities of musical nurture, departmental growth and development, funerals, weddings, or worship planning. It is unlikely that the artist will attend midweek services or Bible study unless there is a special guest or a highly publicized service. Although music can and should undergird and reaffirm Christian education, musicians or staff other than the artist in residence are left with fulfilling this responsibility.

The second new category is the *minister for youth and music, the minister of Christian education and music*, or the *church administrator and music director*. This person serves the church part-time as a musician and part-time as a youth minister, Christian education director, or church administrator. From 9:00 A.M. to 5:00 P.M. Monday through Friday, this person answers the phone, tends to clerical details, runs errands, and administers other aspects of the church's ministries. He or she may sing and play for funerals and may even help in the kitchen. In the evenings and sometimes on Saturdays, these staff members rehearse the choir, play for weddings, revivals, and special services, and go to engagements at other churches. Some of these musicians find time to teach private piano lessons. This employee is overworked, tired, and unable to do either job well because of the overwhelming responsibilities related to each. However, churches feel that they can justify a full-time salary if one person has all of these duties and responsibilities.

The third new category is the *gifted and talented gospel musician*, who can perform only contemporary gospel music but is given the title "minister of music" and placed in charge of the music program. This musician does not read music and often is younger than the people he or she must lead. If hymns are used in the service, they are all gospelized. The choir is trained by rote, and all music is learned from CDs, even in rehearsals. What is popular on the radio and *Billboard* charts determines the selection of music for the choir and congregation.

It is also possible to define church musicians by the extent of their involvement, as N. Lee Orr does:

> The *transitional church musician* is the least involved of the three types. He or she typically enters and leaves the field of church music several times and combines this career with other types of employment or raising a family.
>
> The phrase *part-time church musician* covers a broad area as to almost defy definition. . . . Many part-time church musicians (those who teach school or give private music lessons) direct an adult choir, children's choir, bell choir, and play the organ. While their job (and salary!) is described as part-time, the energy requirements--the time spent thinking, worrying, praying--easily approach forty hours a week.
>
> The critical difference between the *full-time* and part-time church musician does not lie in musical training, commitment to the position, or quality of music on Sunday morning. Rather the full-time position means that the musician is at the church every day, as well as rehearsals, Sundays, and extra services. Supposedly, compensation including benefits (which the part-time position rarely has) for the full-time position is commensurate with the time involved.[2]

The supply and demand for musicians is so critical that many churches are willing to settle for musicians who can play by ear in C, F, and G, and B flat on Easter. Churches would rather have somebody play the piano or organ than to sing a cappella. If another church offers that same musician fifty or a hundred dollars more, the musician will soon leave. Many high-school and first- and second-year college students who have had no training, mentoring, or previous experience in church music are asked to assume the leadership role in churches and are paid significantly.

By contrast, other churches have musicians who have served past their usefulness and are unwilling to cooperate with changing trends and worship styles. Many of them have more authority than the pastor because of their tenure in the church. These musicians have served for forty or more years and proudly proclaim their sovereignty in the church. They have not varied their repertoire, polished their skills, practiced their instrument, or read anything current in church music in the last twenty-five years. They have tremendous influence over the choir and church leaders, and in most instances they will not work with the pastor. The church and choir must endure repetition, musical inaccuracies, and repertoire that is outdated and out of the range of the current choir.

Many churches have musicians who have been trained in music education, voice, piano, choral conducting, music theory, and composition and teach in public schools, colleges, and universities. However, they have never taken courses in liturgy, worship, hymnody, biblical studies, or theology. They impose the repertoire from their schools and many times treat adults in the choir like their adolescent students.

Challenges and Opportunities for Musicians

There is a growing realization that traditional classical training has not prepared musicians for leadership in the late twentieth- and twenty-first-century African American church. The classical western European model remains the standard for collegiate education, and little if any consideration is given to the musical history and worship traditions and practices of the African American religious experience. Musicians rely on their experiences and what is popular as a guide for selecting and performing music in the church.

Some black colleges and universities, seminaries, denominations, local churches, and other institutions are developing effective means for musicians to retool their skills. These means include continuing education classes, private instrumental and vocal study, books, videos, and conferences. Churches should require that their musicians participate in these opportunities for growth and change, and churches should provide funding.

No matter what size congregation a church musician serves, the work necessitates extensive preparation. Congregations, even the smallest ones, want the best choral direction, the most exciting instrumental music, and the most inspiring worship music possible.[3] Regardless of the categories of musicians in our churches, the common factor should be to strive for excellence. Excellence honors God! Harold M. Best writes,

> Excellence is the process—note the word *process*—of becoming better than I once was. I am not to become better than someone else is or even like someone else. Excelling is simply—and radically—the process of improving over yesterday or, in the apostle Paul's words, "pressing on" (Philippians 3:14, NIV).
>
> Whatever the standards or conditions are, I am to strive to better them and to seek higher ones. In fact, I might even be able to raise the ones that exist.[4]

Striving for excellence needs to be tempered with realistic expectations, as Rory Noland cautions:

> Setting goals can be motivational and can bring significant growth. Even if we don't achieve all our goals, we're almost always better off for having tried. Now contrast that with constantly browbeating ourselves and others because we're not living up to perfection.... If you and I set unrealistic expectations, we're setting ourselves up for frustration and disappointment every time. That's why perfectionists live with a lot of "if onlys." ... People with unrealistic expectations often end up sabotaging themselves.... We need to work hard and aim high, but a perfect performance or a perfect life is an unrealistic goal that is more man-centered than God-centered. I think *perfection* should be spelled with an i in the middle instead of an e, because perfection really is "perfiction." It's pure fantasy to envision ourselves as perfect.[5]

Church musicians should never confuse excellence with perfection. However, we must always seek higher ground. The hymn writer exhorts, "My prayer, my aim is higher ground!"

CHAPTER THREE

ESSENTIALS FOR CHURCH MUSICIANS

THE FIRST AND FOREMOST REQUIREMENT FOR A CHURCH musician is to love the Lord God with all one's heart and one's entire mind. If musicians do not first love God and the people of God, all their talents, skills, and training will not help them to succeed. A pastor once told me, "I'm looking for a musician for my church, and the first thing I want to know is, does that person love the Lord?" Although this seems basic and simple, in many instances musicians talk church talk but refuse to walk church walk. Just as ministers are called of God, so, I am persuaded, church musicians are called of God. "There must be a distinction between *musicians at churches* and *church musicians*," Wyatt Tee Walker points out. "The profile is straightforward: he/she must be born again, subscribe to the tithing principle, study the Scriptures in specific regimen, [be] thoroughly professional in conduct and [understand] the concept of collegial leadership. This profile is precisely necessary to pastors too."[1]

Distinctive Requirements for Church Musicians
The requirements and qualifications for church musicians have been laid out by many authors but are worth reviewing. Kenneth W. Osbeck argues that musicians serve a holy God and then lists ten conditions for musicians that the Old Testament records:

> *Especially chosen from the Levitical priesthood*—not just anyone could serve in this capacity (1 Chron. 15:1,2; 11-22; 16:4-7; 37:41, 42; 2 Chron.20:21; Neh. 7:1).

Well organized—they were assigned specific work and were individually appointed to their tasks (2 Chron. 7:6; 8:14; 31:2; Neh. 11:2).

Educated and trained—teachers as well as scholars (1 Chron. 15:22; 25:1-8; Neh. 11:22; 12:42,46).

Efficient performers—punctual and systematic. Note the word "skillful" is used of them often (1 Chron. 16:37; 2 Chron. 8:14; 15:22; 31:2).

Consecrated—that is, they were to have clean hands and pure hearts (Num. 8:5-16; 1 Chron. 15:12,14,16; 2 Chron. 5:11,12).

Models of obedience to God's Word (2 Chron. 34:30-32).

Set apart by wearing distinctive robes (1 Chron. 15:27; 2 Chron. 5:12).

Recognized and paid for their services (Num. 18:21; 2 Chron. 31:2-10; Neh. 12:47; 13:5,10,11). Homes were to be provided for them as well (Ezra 2:70; Neh. 7:73; 12:28,29).

Treated as other religious leaders—with no discrimination (Ezra 7:24; Neh. 10:28,29,39).

Mature (only those aged thirty and over). This was not a service to be performed by the young and inexperienced (Num. 4:47; 1 Chron. 23:3-5). [2]

In addition to possessing natural gifts and talents, skills, and musicianship, church musicians must love the Word of God so much that they become lifelong students of the Word. Musicians must also love the church and seek to understand its history and development from the origins of Christianity to the local history of the church that they serve. Paul Westermeyer best summarizes this need:

"Church" brings with it the thought of what the church is engaged in, usually called theology, which reflects on and has implications for music and everything else in its life. Since the central documents of that theology are the Old and New Testaments, biblical study is necessary. There is a history of what the church has done as well as what it has thought, so history is important. Worship has been the focus in the life of the church and the point where music is most directly involved, so liturgical studies must be included. The church has been concerned about education, and music is tied to that concern, so Christian education cannot be forgotten. The church has a mission, so evangelism and ethics are present, though they could fit under the broader heading of theology as well. Hymnology, first the study of the hymn texts and then the music that clothes those texts, can be included as a separate category, though it could be subsumed under liturgical studies. All the categories could be subdivided: history, for example, into the periods of the Old and New Testaments and then early, medieval, Reformation, and Modern church history; theology into branches such as systematic, practical, pastoral, missional, and ethical.[3]

These points should also guide musicians as they select literature other than that about church music and worship.

And it is of utmost importance that church musicians read! Serious church musicians read classics, such as *Music Leadership in the Church* by Eric Routley and *Music and Worship in the Church* by Austin C. Lovelace and William C. Rice. But they also read current literature and enquire about new and reliable writings. Resources addressing the duties, responsibilities, calling, role, and mission of the musician have nearly tripled over the past few decades. Some of the finest resources, and those most helpful to me, include *The Church Musician* by Paul Westermeyer, *The Church Music Handbook for Pastors and Musicians* by N. Lee Orr, and *Ministry and Musicians* by William L. Hooper. Or a musician might consult *Things They Didn't Tell Me about Being a Minister of Music* by C. Harry Causey and *Things They Never Tell You Before You Say "Yes"* by Robin Knowles Wallace. *The Musician's Soul* by James Jordan and *The Heart of the Artist* by Rory Noland address spiritual aspects of a musician's life and work. For other insights one might read *An ABC Primer for Church Musicians* by Bob Burroughs or *Trouble at the Table* by Carol Doran and Thomas H. Troeger.

Typical Responsibilities of Church Musicians
Regardless of the size of the congregation, numerous variables shape time requirements for a church musician. Among these variables are the number and size of choirs, the difficulty of the

repertoire, seasonal liturgies, and the level of congregational expectations. The following checklist, which was adapted from a chapter of the American Guild of Organists (AGO), outlines the variety of responsibilities and duties that come with leadership positions in the field of sacred music.[4]

MUSIC
Selection of Music
1. Choosing appropriate repertoire for organ and choirs from current library.
2. Choosing appropriate new repertoire for organ and choirs from new publications and editions.
3. Selection of service music.

Preparation of Repertoire
1. Personal practice time.
2. Personal study time for preparing and learning repertoire for the organ and choir(s).

Rehearsal of Repertoire
1. Keyboard practice time.
2. Schedule choir rehearsals.
3. Organ setup, rehearsal, and organization prior to weekly service.
4. Choir warm-up rehearsals prior to service.

Services
1. Weekly services.
2. Holy days, concerts, and other special events.

ADMINISTRATION
Staff Meetings
1. Worship planning team, pastoral staff, music staff.
2. Music committee, congregational committee on music and liturgy.
3. Special events committees.

Music Program Development
1. Recruitment of singers and other musicians.
2. Planning with music staff, parent assistants, secretarial help, and other volunteers.
3. Fundraising events.
4. Choir retreats.

Music Library
1. Stamping and filing
2. Inventory and cataloging, manual and database.
3. Organizing volunteer help.

Maintenance
1. Personal maintenance of instruments (organs, pianos, handbells, etc.) and other equipment (e.g., music stands, stand lights).
2. Supervision of contracted maintenance of organs, pianos, and other instruments.
3. Synthesizer and recording equipment setup.
4. Rehearsal and performance setup.
5. Choir robe cleaning and repair.

Budget
1. Music for choirs, piano, and organ.
2. Maintenance for organs, pianos, and equipment.
3. Payroll for music staff and guest artists.
4. Long-range goals, including purchasing instruments and planning major concerts.
5. Projecting future needs.

Written Communications
1. Church newsletter or bulletin.
2. Press releases and community publicity.
3. Personal correspondence with professional colleagues and church members.
4. Request for permission to use protected material.

CONTINUING EDUCATION
1. Private keyboard study and/or vocal training.
2. Attendance at professional workshops, clinics, conferences,and conventions at local, state, and national levels.
3. Membership in national, state, and local professional organizations, such as the American Guild of Organists, American Choral Directors Association, Choristers Guild,
   American Guild of English Handbell Ringers, and in
   various denominational organizations.

Some activities of the church musician, such as worship services
and rehearsals, are highly visible to the congregation. Much more
of the work, including practicing, administration, and selection and
preparation of music, is not seen by others but is necessary for a
quality music program.

Congregations require different kinds and levels of skill from
their professional musicians, and their programs emphasize different
areas of expertise. For instance, in some situations sight reading and
keyboard improvisation skills are paramount. In other cases ability
in composition and arranging is essential. Other positions give priority to knowledge of the liturgy and repertoire of a particular
denomination.

The well-prepared church musician must have a strong background in performance, preferably organ, piano, and/or voice. In
addition, the musician must be skilled in conducting, both choral
and instrumental; theory and sight singing; and arranging, for both
choral and instrumental ensembles. The church musician must
know the music of the church, including choral music, hymnody,
and instrumental resources; music history, specifically the different
eras and styles of sacred music; and the theology and history of the
church and its mission.[5]

This variety of functions challenges any church musician, and
other skills such as ministry, organization, and administration
are also critical to building a successful music program. Weak
musicianship, inattention to details, or difficulty in working with
people can undermine a musician's effectiveness. The smaller the

church, the more critical all of these skills become, because there are fewer resources for the church musician.

In his summary of the church musician's functions, Orr includes many categories similar to those in the list from the AGO. But Orr adds two new, significant points (the eighth and tenth ones):

Preparing and performing music for worship

General program administration

Conducting and/or playing

Selecting music

Studying and preparing music for rehearsal

Rehearsing the choir

Recruiting choir members

Working effectively with pastor and congregation

Maintain musical skills

Shepherding choir members[6]

A slightly different perspective comes from Causey, who reminds us that a church musician has to be a politician, be married to the job, be a financial wizard, be a psychologist, be a producer, be a Bible scholar, be a servant, be an administrator, be a personality, and be a disciplinarian.[7] These are the realities of the church musician, choir director, or minister of music.

Defining the Role for a Minister of Music

James Robert Davidson defines a minister of music as "the person who combines the tasks of ministry and music leadership . . . and is often ordained to the ministry with music as the tool of his calling. This role includes the gathering of the people, the teaching of them, and the caring for them through a musical dimension within the total redemptive-creativity activity." He explains that the term "is relatively recent to church music having appeared around the mid-twentieth century among evangelical Protestant churches in America. A real impetus toward its use came from the Southern Baptist Convention with its establishment of the Department of Church Music (1941) as a part of the Sunday School Board and its implementation of Schools of Church Music in the various seminaries." An even more important difference, says Davidson, is that

> unlike the director of music, the minister of music is involved with more than simply choral and instrumental ensembles and leading the congregational singing. He is concerned with the total congregation, what the needs are of the congregation as individuals, and what music will best meet the needs, and effect a desired response. Through his choice and use of music, he is involved in the process of instilling theological concepts as well as a devotional vocabulary. His ability to know his congregation and individual attitudes, to identify with these, and to provide the catalyst for a feeling of community in the proclamation of Christian truth through music comprise the discipline and limits of his work.[8]

Although this definition does not reflect what many ministers of music do, it is a model to which we can aspire. Some churches refer to this person as the director of music, the music coordinator, or the choir director. The main issue is the specific role of that musician for that situation. The title assigned to the musician should be accompanied by a comprehensive, explicit job description for the position. It must be clear what is expected, what is required, and what method of evaluation will be used to assess those expectations and requirements better known as duties and responsibilities. They will not be the same for every church.[9]

Before earthshaking forces began to transform the church during the 1960s, there was an acknowledged right way to fulfill the role of church musician. However, there is no longer a generic right way but rather *many* right ways. The role now requires that musicians seek to determine what is appropriate for the particular occasion in which a particular congregation gathers to worship.[10] This decision involves interrelated and sometimes conflicting needs, including the church's tradition, the ever-expanding repertoire of congregational songs, what resources are available, current history, acoustics, liturgical developments within the denomination, the state of the relationship with the pastor and worship committee, the pastoral needs of the community, and the kind of musical leadership that is available among the people.[11]

Finally, what is true for pastors is true for musicians. It is inadequate preparation for their ministries to be trained only within the limits of their disciplines. Musical excellence is essential to the successful practice of the discipline, but Doran and Troeger suggest that the musician

> must have an understanding of the communal forces and tension that are present in the congregation and how these often converge around the worship service and its music; a perspective on how music serves to awaken prayer and ministry of people, even those who are not gifted musically but who still have a need to sing their Creator's praise; the ability to handle conflict . . . an attitude of flexibility that balances one's sense of artistic standards with the realities of a congregation's limits and needs; a sense of what it means to be a colleague with the pastor so planning the leadership of worship can be a collaborative effort; and the spiritual grace to communicate through one's leadership how music is a gift from and a witness to the One who is the source of all that is true and beautiful.[12]

When these essentials are in place, then and only then will Mt. Zion truly rejoice!

CHAPTER FOUR

THE RELATIONSHIP BETWEEN PASTORS AND MUSICIANS

N 1986 I HAD THE PRIVILEGE OF HAVING AN EXTENSIVE conversation with the late Reverend James Cleveland, king of gospel music and pastor of the Cornerstone Institutional Baptist Church in Los Angeles. Because as a child he was a constant companion to his grandmother, Annie, she carried him to the worship services and choir rehearsals at the Pilgrim Baptist Church in Chicago. James was fondly known as the mascot of the choir, which then was under the direction and tutelage of the father of gospel, Thomas A. Dorsey.

As a young boy, Cleveland began to nurture his God-given talent for singing and playing the piano. He eventually became a member of the Mahalia Jackson Singers, the Thorne Crusaders, the Gospel Allstars of New York, the Roberta Martin Singers, the Caravans of Chicago, and the Meditation Singers. In Detroit he developed the Radio Choir at the New Bethel Baptist Church, pastored by the late Reverend C. L. Franklin, where he was first the baby-sitter and then the tutor for the piano lessons of the Reverend Franklin's daughter Aretha. After many successful years as a gospel songwriter, singer, and musician, Cleveland was called to the ministry, and in November 1970 he organized and stepped forth as pastor of the Cornerstone Church.

When I asked him what he thought to be the most critical problem with music in the African American church, the Reverend Cleveland quickly responded, "The pastor and musician learning to work together and get along. You know they both have big egos that get in the way, and that what's wrong everywhere I go."

I asked the same question for my dissertation at the University of Michigan. The majority of my respondents were pastors and musicians who had served as musicians in churches before they became pastors. These respondents included the Reverend Andrae Crouch, pastor of the Christ Memorial Church of God in Christ in Pacoima, California; the Reverend Marvin Winans, pastor of the Perfecting Church in Detroit; Bishop Paul S. Morton, pastor of the Greater Stephens Baptist Church in New Orleans and founder of the Full Gospel Baptist Convention, Inc.; and the Reverend Dr. Jeremiah A. Wright Jr., pastor of the Trinity United Church of Christ in Chicago. They agreed that the relationship between pastors and musicians is critical.

"It will remain bad theology so long as the theologian and the artist refuse to communicate with one another, as long as the theologian regards the artist as fundamentally a temperamental trifler, and the theologian as an obstinate and ignorant theorist, the best we shall get is patronage from church to music, together with tentative moralisms from musicians to musicians," Eric Routley wrote in his classic, *Church Music and Theology.* "At worst it will be, as it often in practice is, a wicked waste of an opportunity for glorifying God through fruitful partnership."[1] And, if we substitute the word *pastor, minister,* or *priest* for "theologian" and the term *musician* or *choir director* for "artist," these comments are still relevant.

In the ideal situation, the pastor will select the music director or minister of music. While, as noted in chapter 3, it is true that the musician serves the congregation and needs to be able to get along with a variety of people (including the music committee, choir, deacons, trustees, etc.), it is the pastor with whom the musician must work closely on a weekly basis. Thus, although music committees may present candidates, the final decision should rest with the pastor. In 1 Chronicles 15, David assembled the Levites and asked the chief of the Levites to appoint men to be singers and instrumentalists. Heman, Asaph, and Ethan were appointed to sound the cymbals of brass. Kenaniah, chief of the Levites, was selected for songs because he instructed about the songs and was skillful. This text clearly tells me that the pastor should select the chief musician, and the chief musician should appoint other musicians according to their abilities and skills. As we know, the Levites had to be consecrated, anointed, cleansed, and skilled.

Developing a Partnership

It is unfortunate that pastors and musicians in so many churches give little if any time to developing a strong and fruitful partnership. In some worship services the pastor takes one path and the musician takes another, and there is little evidence of any communication about the service. Sunday after Sunday the congregation must endure liturgical collisions and digest casseroles of unrelated topics and elements in worship.

The worshipers wonder, What in the world are we doing? Why didn't they talk about this before now? It is distracting, disengaging, and confusing when the sermon, Scriptures, and music are not related. It is devastating when, after a wonderful sermon, a musician selects an invitational hymn, choir piece, or solo that is unrelated and destroys the message or puts out the fire. This happens so frequently that most Sundays the congregation expects "Just As I Am," "I Surrender All," "Come to Jesus," "Amazing Grace," "Softly and Tenderly," or "I Have Decided to Follow Jesus," regardless of what the minister has preached.

Although the pastor is the chief shepherd and executive officer of the church, he or she must be willing to abdicate an autocratic attitude, open up to dialogue, and "move from pride to partnership," a phrase coined by Don Wardlaw. Successful partnerships begin with understanding, and productive partnerships rely on quality communication. Many people confuse talking with communicating. People think that the more they talk, the better they are communicating. But good communication begins when we stop talking and listen. Much of the time we can improve our communication skills by listening more. Talking at people means we not only miss what they are saying but also risk misunderstanding their point of view. We then leave the encounter further convinced of how right we are, which hardens our position.[2] It is no wonder that the other person is not enthusiastic or optimistic about future dialogue.

Four ways to improve communication between pastor and musician, says N. Lee Orr, are to make no assumptions, to check out things before acting, to learn to listen, and to use reason rather than emotion.[3] This essential partnership may be strengthened by genuinely understanding each other, being dependable, and learning how to negotiate. Learning to negotiate is challenging but can be achieved by following these steps:

1. Focusing on the problem, not the person.
2. Staying open to other ideas, not arriving with a closed mind.
3. Listening genuinely, not simply waiting until it is your turn to speak.
4. Remaining flexible, not stating things in absolute terms.
5. Staying committed to the process, not retreating when things become difficult.[4]

Successful partnerships require more than following the suggestions in this or any other book. Affirming a partnership needs broader participation than interacting correctly and avoiding mistakes. Working partnerships between ministers and musicians result when both parties actively support the other, avoid public criticism of the other, ignore minor irritants, and work toward building a friendship.[5]

Understanding Each Other's Perspective

Pastor and musician need to possess a rudimentary knowledge of the suppositions, skills, and vocabulary of each other's discipline. Without this knowledge communication and partnership become difficult or even impossible, and even the best-intentioned efforts at collaborative ministry become strained.[6] "Clergy who have had excellent instruction in pastoral care often lack any sense of how to converse in a professional way with one of the single most important colleague in their ministry: the church musician." But, Carol Doran and Thomas H. Troeger continue, "the story works in reverse as well: the musician, inexperienced in discussing theology and often feeling powerless, is fearful of beginning a conversation with the pastor about the way music functions in the liturgy. Sometimes musicians view their contribution entirely from the perspective of performance without considering how it fits with the liturgical and pastoral needs of the congregation."[7]

The quintessential pastor and musician possess a common vision of their task and a sufficient understanding of each other's vocabulary and perspective. If the two lack a common vocabulary and vision, the church's worship life suffers, and it is a rare Sunday when people experience unity and being of one accord. Then the finest preaching and the most polished and spirited singing and playing cannot redeem the situation. The first redemptive means to expand our thinking about theology and music, Doran and Troeger believe, is to develop a more positive appreciation for the nonverbal dimensions of the Word (*logos*) and to understand music as a pastoral art.

Wyatt Tee Walker offers a slightly different perspective on the issue when he says,

> If I may, let me suggest that our theme is redundant and/or imprecise. It is the questionable legacy and tradition of preachers doing the preaching and musicians doing the music! There needs to be a clear understanding on the basis of Biblical tradition that music is ministry just as preaching is ministry. Until that becomes a given in the African American Church arena, nothing much is going to change for the better. Pastor and Choir Director/Minister of Music/Organist must be partners for Christ's sake. . . . Pastors and Musical Directors must face the reality that when we approach the task of preparing to lead the Lord's people in worship, we need to check our egos at the door. This idea of turf . . . is counter productive to that which is our central mission—leading folks to Christ.[8]

The musician ought to be able to take the minister's subject and sermon text and provide music that will complement, reinforce, and support the message. A general knowledge of Scripture is a must, as is knowledge of a repertoire that will enhance the message. When the musician does this, the congregation is inspired, educated, and lifted through both the sermon and the music, which serves as a handmaiden or servant of the spoken Word. When the minister and musician work together, worship can be a glorious experience. Their fruitful, harmonious collaboration blesses the congregation.

Musicians commonly complain that ministers do not know what their sermons will be until late that week and sometimes not until Sunday morning. If this is the case, the musician must have the music well planned according to the Christian Year and the lectionary; then unity is not lost in what the minister and the musicians attempt to present. Pastors who use the lectionary and observe the Christian Year have a tremendous advantage because the Scriptures and the themes guide musical selections.

One of the most valuable tools for musicians and pastors in selecting hymns to coincide with Scriptures and the minister's sermon is Donald A. Spencer's *Hymn and Scripture Selection Guide*. This work lists alphabetically forty-two of the most frequently used hymns with corresponding Scripture references. It includes publication dates and names of composers and more than twenty-five hundred topical entries. Many other handbooks for the Christian Year and the *Revised Common Lectionary* (see chap. 10) are also available, a number of which are listed in this book's bibliography.

Improving the Relationship

Although weekly meetings are ideal, a monthly meeting of the music staff with the pastor and other worship leaders is the minimum. Regular meetings allow staff to evaluate the past and plan for future worship experiences. Coming together allows interaction, critique, compliments, and challenges to be presented in an environment that provides for growth. The meetings should always begin with the positive aspects of the worship service, move to constructive evaluation, and then review the negative aspects. Pastors and musicians owe it to the congregation—the people who pay their salaries—to meet regularly and plan for the gathering on the Lord's Day.

One of the questions for my dissertation was, What can be done to improve the relationship between the minister and musician? "Three things: commitment, communication, and consecration," replied the Reverend Dr. Frank Madison Reid, pastor of Bethel African Methodist Episcopal Church in Baltimore. "I think that the relationship at best should be that of a good marriage. . . . Instead of there being a commitment as spiritual partners, we become jealous of 'why did you have them shouting over there and not have us shouting over here this Sunday?' This brings about antagonism and resentment. . . . Constant communication fosters the partnership. Finally, prayer and fasting should be a part of the spiritual life of both the minister and musician and should be shared as an ongoing part of the partnership—consecration, that is."9

Pastors and musicians must purpose in their hearts to have a genuine, consistent partnership for the sake of the mission that is much bigger than either of the two individuals. This is easier said than done, but it must be a priority if Mt. Zion is to rejoice!

CHAPTER FIVE

CHOIRS IN THE CHURCH

I
N THE AFRICAN AMERICAN CHURCH, NO GROUP OR organization is more visible and audible than the choir. Its history reaches into the nineteenth century; "as black churches began to emerge after the Civil War, church choirs were organized," writes J. Wendell Mapson Jr. "However, this development was not without conflict. These choirs represented a wide spectrum of music, from choirs steeped in the tradition of the Fisk Jubilee Singers to note-singing (using do-re-mi) choirs and quartets in the deep South. It is essential to understand that among the black masses particularly, the black church became the center of community activity. Music became an important function and the church became, among other things, a kind of entertainment center. To some extent, the congregation became the audience, the pulpit a stage, and the folk preacher and choir the entertainers."[1]

"[C]hoirs have elected officers, purchased music and robes, conducted special events, and participated in visits and exchanges too numerous to count," according to Floyd Massey Jr. and Samuel B. McKinney. "These activities have not only enriched the church but also have created another arena for participatory growth for its constituents."[2]

In the African American church one typically will find at least five or six choirs, even if the church only has one hundred members. Probably no other church boasts about the number of its choirs. Several years ago, when I was being interviewed for a job as a church musician, the pastor proudly announced that the church had ten choirs. On the Sunday I attended, the Men's Chorus sat in one choir loft, the Women's Chorus sat in the other, and a youth ensemble of approximately twelve singers sat on the front pew. Each choir had its own director and musician. At the end of the service, two and half hours later, the senior pastor asked my opinion of the music and service. I did not mention the length of the service, but I hesitantly and reluctantly shared my concern about the quality of singing for the quantity of singing groups. He laughed and agreed but quickly informed me that the Women's Chorus reported between eight and ten thousand dollars a year to his anniversary. Needless to say, I didn't take that job.

Numbers of Choirs and Musical Genres

Graded choir programs usually include preschool children (ages 3-5), primary (ages 6-8), junior (ages 9-11), middle school or junior high (ages 12-14, which music educators agree present the greatest challenge), high school (ages 15-18), an adult choir, and senior or seasoned adults. By contrast, most African American churches have a choir for children and/or youth, a male chorus, a gospel choir, a senior choir, and the mass choir that sings on the first or fifth Sundays and for special events. The mass choir is made of delegates from all of the choirs and usually totals fewer members than any one choir. Note that I said the average African American church. The larger churches have five to eight adult choirs. The names may be Senior Choir no. 1, Senior Choir no. 2, the Inspirational Chorus or Gospel Chorus, the Chorus Choir, the Reverend A. B. C. Goodshepherd Memorial Choir, the Jubilee Chorus, the Cathedral Choir, the Women's Chorus, the Male Chorus, the Gospel Ever Readies, the Temple Singers, the Voices of Praise, the Angelic Voices, and so on. The Reverend Marvin Winans, pastor of the Perfecting Church in Detroit, told me that he has two adult choirs in his church—the Perfecting Praise, which is the auditioned choir, and the Joyful Noise, which does not require auditions and is for anyone who wants to sing.

It is understandable that churches that have two and three services each Sunday need choirs and singers for these services. However, the norm is that one choir sings on the first and third

Sundays, one choir sings on the second Sunday, and the children and youth sing on the fourth or fifth Sunday. This means there will be a different congregation depending on the choir and singers participating in the service. The congregation from the first and third Sundays rarely meets the congregations from the second and fourth Sundays, except on special occasions when their favorite choir or guest preacher is in town.

One might expect each group to sing different styles or genres of music, but in most cases they all sing gospel music. One choir may sing traditional gospel, while the other sings contemporary gospel. One choir sings the fast gospel, while the other sings the slow gospel. One choir sings homemade gospel, while the other sings the Top Forties gospel hits. One choir has to sing whatever the musician can play and teach, while the other choir has several musicians and directors who teach what they like and what they know.

What is lacking in most situations is a well-balanced group of singers. That is, Senior Choir no. 1 may have twelve sopranos, sixteen altos, three tenors, and one bass, a man who sings the melody two octaves lower. The Male Chorus has eight first tenors, four second tenors, two baritones, and seven basses who sing in two-and-half-part harmony. And that is not to say that all of the singers have strong, reliable voices. One would think that it would be logical for the two groups to combine to form a better group, but that is unlikely. The men enjoy doing everything else with the women but singing with them in church! Many choir directors cannot get men to join the mixed chorus.

Historically, Senior Choir no. 1, the Chancel Choir, or the Sanctuary Choir has sung the anthems, hymns, and arranged concert spirituals. Senior Choir no. 2, the Gospel Chorus, or the Inspirational Chorus has sung gospel. Many people disagree, and I respect their position, but I find that assigning specific genres to certain choirs creates dissension and competition. This circumstance violates the apostle Paul's mandate: "Let the word of Christ dwell in you richly as you teach and admonish one another with all wisdom, and as you sing psalms, hymns and spiritual songs with gratitude in your hearts to God" (Colossians 3:16, NIV). The mandate does not suggest that one organize a choir for each genre.

"As the black community turned inward to find meaning in its own institutions," Mapson tells us, "there emerged within the black church some of the same sociological characteristics already existing in the outside world. Because the masses of black people were ill equipped to compete in the larger society, competition developed within the black church and particularly within choirs. Today most black churches have several choirs. . . . As a result of this elaborate choir structure within the church there is a tendency toward competitiveness: choirs vie for popularity and prestige. Each choir, adorned in its own color and style of robe, may even boast of having its own organist and its own particular Sunday to sing. Many choir members are more faithful to their choir than they are to the total ministry of the church."[3]

Musical Styles and Preferences

One of the most powerful weapons that Satan continues to use to attack the Christian church is the explosive issue of musical styles. Many churches are fighting and buzzing with anxious, fevered discussions of the subject. Others have already divided in order to meet the differing preferences of the congregation, some by scheduling contrasting services at different hours and others by establishing a new church. As heaven's first minister of music, Lucifer knew the power of music in praising and worshiping God, and over the years he has been successful in dividing, distracting, and destroying God's people with the style wars. One of the greatest causes of segregation, competition, discord, and quarrelling in our churches is not over how many souls are being won to Christ but among the choir as to who can out-sing who and who can get the house with what song and with what soloist leading the song! Satan has to get a good laugh at us as he observes the choir impersonating a unified body of singers, descendants of the Levites and ministers of music who worship and praise God.

In *I Don't Like That Music*, Robert H. Mitchell asks six essential questions about any style of sacred music: Is it scriptural? Is it traditional? Is it good music? Is it comfortable? Are they good texts and tunes? Are they comfortable?[4] I strongly recommend Mitchell's work for churches that are struggling with the questions Why don't we sing the good old hymns anymore? and Why don't we sing new songs to the Lord?

Fewer adult choirs in the church would provide a more balanced vocal distribution, an expanded repertoire, an increased variety of musical styles offered, an adequately compensated choir director and supporting musicians to produce excellence in music and worship, and a unified music ministry that is less competitive and more focused on ministry. A good church choir should be able to perform all of the music of the church's tradition, which includes anthems, hymns, arranged spirituals, and traditional and contemporary gospel music. In the twenty-first century, a congregation should not have to wait until the first or third Sunday to hear an anthem or the second or fourth Sunday to hear gospel.

Years ago Waldo S. Pratt made an observation that is still true: "The chief cause of trouble about the choir is that its field and its aims are too vaguely defined in the minds of its members, its managers, and the public and the public at large. . . . In default of some basis of principles, we shall find ourselves swayed hither and thither by chance impulses, bewildered by conflicting currents of hasty opinion, and occasionally swept completely off our feet. Happily for the general welfare of the subject, in all of our churches and among most musicians there is a far greater readiness for sound opinions than some good people suppose. In this field, as in others, we may be sure there is everywhere a large amount of diffused, latent commonsense and right feeling to which we may confidently appeal."[5]

The Choir Leads by Example

The role of the choir is to lead the congregation in worship, to represent the congregation, and to instruct the congregation in worship. Another way to consider the choir's role is that it sings to, for, and with the congregation in worship. The first task of the choir is to lead the congregation in worship, and this leadership begins with the choir's first audible or visible activity at the beginning of worship and continues as long as the choir can be seen or heard. Noticeably wandering minds, talking, walking, chewing gum, passing notes, roving eyes, wiggling bodies, and sleeping can distract the congregation and destroy the worship experience. The choir should not be the focus or center of worship, but it should help bring focus to the worship experience. When this role is not clearly understood and accepted by choir members, the church will have singing without commitment, music without meaning, and religious entertainment without reverence and exhortation.

The choir must lead by example, and not only musically. The choir should lead the church in tithing, Bible study, and prayer. How can you lead where you do not go? How can you sing what you don't know? First Corinthians 14:15 (KJV) says, "I will pray with the spirit, and I will pray with the understanding also: I will sing with the spirit, and I will sing with the understanding also." Many choirs sing texts that they have no knowledge of or any personal experience with. Many choirs sit in the loft and sing "What Shall I Render?" as the tithers come forward but at best tip God with a token from time to time. Malachi 3:8 (KJV) says, "Will a man rob God?" but the text also means, "Will a choir rob God?" And choir members are not exempt from Malachi 3:10.

Choir members also need to be in prayer meeting and in Bible study so that they not only sing God's Word but also know God's Word and sing it with power and anointing, which comes from prayer and fasting.

The essential characteristics of a choir are described by Austin C. Lovelace and William C. Rice:

> A dedicated group of people who have joyfully accepted the opportunities provided by the choir for advancing the kingdom of God.
> A leadership group in hymn singing and worship, functioning always as a part of the worshiping congregation.
> A priestly group, whose primary purpose is to strengthen the act of worship by singing portions of the service which the congregation is unable to do quite so effectively.

An organization of people who consider that regular attendance at all choir activities is a vital part of their service to God.
A crusading force, striving always to make the worship service
more beautiful and more valid.
A unifying force in the whole life of the church.

A choir is not

A concert organization established for the purpose of display-
ing individually or collectively the operatic abilities of its
members. Neither is it a display for the director or organist
with concert ambitions.
Maintained as an entertainment and social organization to
which everyone who is anyone must belong. While the social
life is important, it must never interfere with the real function
of the choir.
A part-time group, holding the allegiance of its members on a
basis of personal convenience, and accepting various flimsy
excuses for their occasional attendance.
A group which one condescends to serve, thereby "laying up
treasures in heaven."
An organization of persons who are pleased to help the director or on special occasions.
An organization that increases in size, improves its attendance,
and works with concentrated interest just before Christmas,
Easter, and other "special" events, leaving the remaining services to get along as best they can.
A group of people who may attend rehearsal, and probably
the morning service if an anthem is to be sung, or the choir
featured in some other fashion.
An organization that offers opportunities for any kind of
personal aggrandizement or for the display of temperament
or jealousy.[6]

There are those who use the expression "volunteer choir" as a
justification for these habits, lack of commitment, and addiction

to mediocrity. But one does not volunteer to attend church, to contribute to the budget, or to perform any other act that is less than a just return to God. In the parable of the talents, Jesus was making a statement of cause and effect. If we fail to use our talents and by so doing fail to glorify him, we have sinned.[7] It follows then that "in the musically mature church, the ministry of choir singing is now regarded as a privilege and a trust."[8]

"Volunteer" has an additional implication that is indeed unfortunate, as Joseph Ashton aptly describes: "The shortcomings and deficiencies of the choir are many times excused on the plea that it is volunteer and that therefore a respectable standard of excellence and efficiency for its purpose is not to be required. That its music is distressing and the service is rendered vapid is not duly regarded. Such a plea is, as a matter of fact, totally unworthy of the high function of a service of divine worship."[9]

Six useful recommendations for moving toward more effective choir ministry come from Mapson:

1. For the health and well-being of the total church, it may be advisable to limit membership in the choir to those persons who are members of the church. The church is a whole made up of parts, and because of the interdependent nature of the body of Christ, to limit choir membership may reduce potential friction from those who may not be sensitive to the purposes and goals of the church and its ministry.

2. One of the ways to improve the quality of music in the church is to reduce the number of choirs. Most churches have too many choirs, many of which are unnecessary. . . . To encourage the formation of more choirs in a church is to invite as well as promote competition and confusion.

3. One of the perennial problems in many choirs is the problem of the soloist, which in reality is the problem of the choir. Again, the gift of the individual must be weighed against the needs of the choir as a whole. The soloist does not "own" a song, nor should one or two persons render all of the solos.

However, it is also helpful to recognize that not all choir members are soloists.

4. Churches should provide money in the budget for the operation of the choir since the choir belongs to the church. It is suggested that the church, not the individual choir members, own the choir robes, for the choir robes are church property, just as the choir is church property in the sense of accountability. Choir robes should not be faddish or profane. Their colors should reflect the symbols of Christian faith. . . . The aim of the choir member is not to show self but to engage in collective worship.

5. Choir members must always guard against the temptation to exhibit self. There are many manifestations of excess in the black church. One of the most disturbing is the tendency of many choirs to become exhibitionists and performers. Many soloists thrive on attention received as they parade from front door to back door. Much of this is contrived and artificial.

6. The choirs in the black church of the masses spend much of their time and energy participating in choir anniversaries. The usual format for these annual events is for choirs from local churches to render two or more selections. These choir festivals are frequently in black churches, especially in those whose members feel a greater sense of social and economic disenfranchisement. Such events are entertaining and tend to be competitive as each choir seeks to out-sing and perform other participants.[10]

I certainly underscore all of Dr. Mapson's recommendations for moving toward more effective choir ministry, but I would hasten to add the following:

7. Choir members must clearly understand and take seriously the meaning of *ministry*. Indeed the term "ministry" is so tossed around that it has become something of a buzzword. Choirs must develop a sense of ministry and understand the dichotomy of servitude and leadership in effective ministry. It is easy enough to lead, but to minister means placing oneself at the disposal of others. The meaning of ministry must become incarnate in the mind, life, and activities of each choir member. They must see themselves as an integral part of the total church ministry. They must see themselves as the musical extension of the preacher and the spoken Word—in effect, musical servants of the Word. Each member must see him or herself as an individual "minister of music."

8. The choir director, choir members, and musicians must establish and maintain a personal Bible study and devotional period in their lives, as well as committing to active involvement in the corporate Bible study and prayer meetings of the church. Too often choir members regard themselves as being exempt from Bible study, prayer meeting, Sunday school, and even tithing! The choir should lead the congregation by example and not by song!

9. Occasionally the choir needs to stop singing and examine the text and meaning of what it is that they are really singing. Many choirs sing without understanding and therefore, their song has no power. Two questions should be at the front of every musical selection: First, does it honor God? and second, Is it biblically based and theologically sound? Choir members must know what they are singing!

10. Rehearsals should always be well planned by the director and should begin and end *on time!* Rehearsal should move with a sense of urgency and direction. When rehearsals lag, attention is lost, boredom sets in, and discipline problems may even arise. Where there is no discipline, there can be no serious learning. Don't waste valuable time in rehearsal!

11. Choirs should have a well-defined mission statement that complements the overall mission of the church. That mission statement should answer the questions, Why do we sing? For whom do we sing? What do we sing? What is the ultimate purpose for our existence as a choir? Every choir member should be able to recite that statement on the spot.

12. Finally, a choir must have a desire to grow and develop. "Getting the house," stirring up a shout, applause, and standing ovation from the congregation, and getting a record deal is not what singing is all about in the church. A serious strategic plan for choir growth and development—spiritually, musically, and socially will bring to the group a more serious commitment among existing members and attract others in the congregation to a thriving and mature music ministry. Whether the choir's goals are to increase the membership, to broaden the repertoire to include more diverse musical offerings, to develop sight-reading and basic music fundamental classes, or to provide retreats that address musicianship, spirituality, and purpose, a short- and long-term plan should always be before the group. The choir should have measurable objectives and should be able to accurately assess their progress.

An old preacher once said, "Every Sunday I try to find *new* ways to tell the *old* story." As a choir, we must too find *new* ways to tell the *old* story in song so that it is palatable to the congregation.

Not Conformed to the World

Children's choirs and youth choirs are extremely neglected in our churches. While there are some wonderful programs, the majority of children's and youth choirs leave much to be desired. When our preschoolers and elementary school children sing "Goin' Up Yonder," "Soon and Very Soon," "Down by the Riverside," and "All My Sins Have Been Taken Away," we have robbed them of the opportunity of being children and being able to relate to their understanding of Christ in the world and in their lives. Music should fit the ages of children and should be performed in a range that accommodates the voices of the specific children. We want our children to live, run, play, grow, develop, become educated, and be with us for a while, not have to "go up yonder" at eight or nine years old or have "hard trials and heavy burdens" between the ages of ten and twelve. Mapson is on target when he asserts, "There is a great deal the black church can do to improve the quality of music, beginning with its children. The church has an urgent educational task to train its youth. The church should not allow youth to dictate the type and style of music used."[11]

Young people don't expect or want the church to duplicate or replicate their favorite R&B and hip-hop stars. Adults just think they do. The youth will ultimately choose between the world and the church, but the church does not need to feed them religious imitations of their secular giants and idols in order to get them in the church and to keep them in the church. Most of the youth in church continue to go to clubs and parties on Friday and Saturday nights, and those who manage to make it to church on Sunday need a word from and an encounter with the Lord Jesus Christ. That word needn't be rapped in DMX, Snoop Doggie Dog, L'il Kim, or Ice Cube to get their attention. We must be careful of compromising the gospel of Jesus Christ in an attempt to win souls. Every new trend and fad does not honor God or promote the kingdom of God.

Nor is this issue limited to our young people. I have discovered that many adults think that the church must be attractive to the world by being like the world in order to attract people. Many churches seek to imitate other churches, television evangelists, and megachurch ministries in order to get a crowd. Musicians are guilty of trying to keep the choir singing the Top Forties popular gospel songs in order to compete with other choirs in the church and in the community. This preoccupation does not honor God and has no place in the church and worship of the people of God.

The Old Testament documents a well-organized plan for worship leaders. The choir, members of the tribe of Levi, was consecrated and set aside to be a part of that leadership, and the Levites were supported in that task by the other eleven tribes. The clerical role of the choir is a biblically corroborated practice that is still needed.[12] Pastoral responsibilities influence the priorities governing the choir's ministry, as the following list by Calvin M. Johansson shows. This list is not exhaustive or inflexible, since each church will have a somewhat different approach depending upon the denomination, the size of the church, and the particular vision of its leaders.

To maintain a right attitude toward God, congregation, pastor, music, and musicians.

To support the pastor and staff in prayer, word, and deed.

To enter into worship wholeheartedly. An unenthusiastic choir will infect the assembly with the same attitude.

To be attentive and responsive to every worship leader, whether lector, soloists, preacher, song leader, or celebrant.

To lead in congregational singing of hymns, psalms, and spiritual songs. Such leadership should be with faces, eyes, and heart, as well as with voices.

Service music, such as calls to worship, acclamations, benedictions, versicles, and responses, should be sung with vigor and enthusiasm. Music which is repeated from week to week needs special attention, since it tends to lose freshness.

To be helpful in giving prayers, witness, words of edification, or scriptural admonitions, especially when a general invitation has been given without any ready congregational response. The choir should act as an icebreaker and prompter.

To open up personally to the preached word. Nothing will aid a pastor's sermonic communication more than the example of a choir paying close attention to every word. The assembly will tend to imitate the listeners they see before them. A choir of disinterested, unenthusiastic, unresponsive, sleepy individuals, who feel that because they have finished their "special music" they have no further responsibility, however, grossly misses the point of its ministry. In such a case it would be better to do away with the choir.

To give prayer support at the altar to those who respond to any invitation which might be given by the pastor. It is disconcerting when the choir is oblivious to the Spirit's working and is in a hurry to leave. Instead the choir must use its influence to help to open the congregation to the gentle and unhurried moving of God's Spirit.

To sing any anthem material as deemed appropriate for the service.[13]

Choirs must be systematically and regularly taught their role. The priorities and attitudes we wish to foster need to be normative. They are best learned as the music director carefully shepherds the choir into maturing patterns of worship leadership and as the director expects each choir member to practice these attitudes regularly and well.[14] Choirs tend to take on the personality of their leaders. Therefore the leaders must demonstrate the goals, missions, and objectives of the ministry.

The pastor must nurture a relationship with the choir, since they are coworkers and must lead together in worship. The pastor's personal rapport with the choir greatly enhances its sharing of and identification with the pastor's spiritual vision for the church. Praying together nourishes community. Nothing will so inspire the choir to do its best as the esprit de corps generated by a pastor who genuinely cares about choir members and expects them to shake the rafters of heaven in their quest for the spiritual advancement of the congregation.[15]

Over the past fifteen years, on numerous occasions, I have served as guest organist and director for the Amity Baptist Church in Jamaica, New York. The Reverend Dwight M. Jackson, the pastor there, meets and prays with his deacons and choir every Sunday prior to his leading the procession for morning worship. There is no late or grand pastoral entrance, and there are no late choir members filing into the loft after the procession. This practice reinforces and reaffirms the partnership and unity of worship leaders going into worship. The team effort is both seen and felt among the worshipers, the choir, and the officers of the church. This is a practice that I strongly encourage pastors to model. It works.

When the choir truly joins with the pastor in worship, Mt. Zion will truly rejoice!

CHAPTER SIX

PLANNING WORSHIP

O VER THE PAST THIRTY YEARS WORSHIP HAS BEEN THE TOPIC of countless books, journals, articles, conferences, seminars, workshops, and sermons. Pastors, theologians, liturgical scholars, and others have attempted to define worship and to examine and exegete its biblical and theological foundations. In this age planning worship has become critical. A tremendous increase in resources and materials such as handbooks, hymnal supplements, videos, cassettes, and CDs assists in this planning.

Most of these resources have been written for and by Euro-Americans and their worship styles and traditions. These include the works of James F. White, Robert E. Webber, Don E. Salier, Marva J. Dawn, C. Welton Gaddy, Paul W. Hoon, and Frank C. Senn. African American worship forms the topic of *Come Sunday* (1990) by William B. McCain, *African American Christian Worship* (1993) by Melva Wilson Costen, *Strange Fire* (1996) by J. Wendell Mapson Jr., *Praising in Black and White* (1996) by Brenda Eatman Aghahowa, and *African American Worship* (1998) by Frederick Hilborn Talbot.

The African American Catholic Church has addressed its worship in *This Far by Faith* (1974) and *Plenty Good Room* (1990). Some of the most significant historical surveys of the African American church and its music and worship include Albert Raboteau's *Slave Religion*, Walter F. Pitts's *Old Ship of Zion*, Harry V. Richardson's *Dark Glory*, W. E. B. Du Bois's *The Souls of Black Folk*, and George R. Ricks's *Some Aspects of the Religious Music of the United States Negro*.

Rituals, Not Worship

Many of our African American church leaders—pastors and musicians—have no real understanding of worship. If the minister has had theological training in a seminary or divinity school, it is likely that neither music and worship nor liturgy were required courses of study. Therefore the rituals that are repeated week after week, month after month, and year after year are associated with or defined by that pastor as worship. The truth is that these rituals without reason, ceremonies without content, services without substance, singing without sincerity, music without meaning, prayers without power or purpose, and Scriptures without significance have become outdated, irrelevant, and ineffective for the worshipers, who are at best spectators. When the minister and the musician fail to plan worship the congregation will experience a comedy of errors, a sacred circus, brilliant failures, successful zeros, and a holy hot mess.

Many of our services, says William D. Watley, are "endurance services." Congregations must endure Brother I-Can't-Read, who always does the memorial; Sister Left-My-Glasses-at-Home, who always reads the announcements; Brother Can't-Speak-in-the-Microphone, who always gives the occasion; Sister Needs-to-Get-a-Life, who always acknowledges and welcomes the visitors; and Sister Been-in-the Choir-Thirty-five-Years, who always sings "Precious Lord" and "He Touched Me."[1]

I once witnessed a Sister Forgot-My-Glasses, who was serving as the mistress of ceremonies for a service, become impatient and annoyed when Mrs. Gloria Patri did not come forward after the reading of the responsive Scripture. She immediately called to the organist to stop playing "Glory Be to the Father" until Mrs. Patri made her presentation. Too much repetition of responses, chants, litanies, and hymns tend to render these acts irrelevant, boring, or annoying.

So many churches have ritualized chants and hymns to the point that they are meaningless to the worshipers. For example, "All Things Come of Thee, O Lord" or "Praise God from Whom All Blessings Flow" must be sung after the offertory every Sunday even if the Holy Spirit has poured out anointing on the choral selection. "The Lord Is in His Holy Temple" or "I Was Glad When They Said unto Me" has always been the introit on Sunday morning. The "Gloria Patri no. 3" is always sung after the responsive reading. "Nearer, My God to Thee" has to be sung after the prayer. "Spirit of the Living God" is always the prayer response. "Sweet Hour of Prayer" is always sung before the altar prayer. "The Lord's Prayer" is always sung after the morning prayer. "What Shall I Render?" or "You Can't Beat God Giving" is always sung during the offering. "Holy, Holy, Holy" or "God of Our Fathers" is always the processional hymn on the first Sunday. The Gospel Chorus always processes on "Sign Me Up." We always sing "Sweet, Sweet Spirit" to welcome our visitors. The organist always chimes the hour before service begins so that we will know that it is eight or eleven. Worshipers must endure this week-by-week repetition whether or not they like it or understand it.

Although the invocation is a short prayer that acknowledges and asks for God's presence in the worship, many invocations become as long as the altar or pastoral prayer. The person who is called on gives a sermon from the floor as the invocation. Or the invocation becomes a prayer that asks God to visit Sister Ethel Mae Cravitts at Harper Memorial Hospital on the fourth floor in room 408, bed 2 and then asks blessings for the bereaved families who have lost loved ones in Georgia, South Carolina, Alabama, and Arkansas this week.

There are unfortunate situations in which the church secretary or the person who prepares the weekly bulletin selects the hymns and responsive readings or even makes decisions about who will offer prayer in the service. He or she must type the bulletin and may not be able to reach the minister or the musician; therefore what the secretary knows, likes, or dislikes becomes the determining factor for weekly worship. Many church offices will receive the sermon title and text from the pastor and the musical selections from the musician with no evidence of collaboration. The minister's sermon may focus on faith while the choir sings "Soon Ah Will Be Done" or "Climbing Up the Rough Side of the Mountain."

Styles of Worship

At least three styles of worship are found in African American churches: liturgical, or traditional; free, or contemporary; and blended, or a mixture of traditional and contemporary.

Liturgical worship generally adheres to a strict order of worship known as a ritual or liturgy. It consists of prayers, musical responses by the choir and congregation, Scripture readings, litanies of prayer, supplication, and dedication, listening to the Word of God, and communion and baptism once a month. In some churches the liturgy is based on the high points of the Christian Year of Advent, Christmas(tide), Epiphany, Lent, Holy Week, Easter(tide), Ascension, and Pentecost, which are saving events in the life and ministry of the Lord Jesus Christ.

Free worship, first practiced by the early followers of Christ, is an informal, structure-free service that reacts against meaningless traditions, customs, and rituals. In its services the worship leader is free to add, subtract, and move the usual elements of worship as he or she sees fit.

Blended worship attempts to bring together traditional and contemporary worship by incorporating various elements from each tradition.

Whether worship is liturgical or free, there are dangers and critical considerations to be recognized in planning. Some of the most prevalent ones, says John F. Wilson, are these:

Liturgical Worship

Too much organization may tend to prohibit the free working of the Holy Spirit.

Too little active participation may make the worshiper nothing more than a spectator.

Too much week-by-week repetition may render the acts of worship meaningless.

Too much reliance upon prescribed texts may prohibit special emphases often desired in the local church.

Free Worship
Too little organization may cause a loss of continuity of worship.
Too much participation may detract from the worshiper's inner reflection and thought.
Too much informality could become distracting and confusing.
Too little organization of messages may lead to overemphasis on favorite themes and sermon texts and a neglect of other important ones.[2]

In the African American church the phrase "having church" refers to a spirit-filled, God-present, anointed outpouring of the Holy Spirit. The genius of black worship is its openness to the creative power of God that frees and enables people, regardless of denomination, to turn themselves loose and celebrate God's act in Jesus Christ.[3] "Indeed, traditional African American worship can be viewed as a spiritual art form," writes Melva Wilson Costen. "The drama inherent in worship lends itself naturally to joyful glorification and enjoyment of God. This is *not* to say that *all* Black worship is designed to be entertaining, nor are all worship experiences filled with physical excitement. Stereotyping of worship undermines mission and ministry, so important in the black community."[4]

Too often the worship of African Americans is considered entertainment, amusing, jammin' and slammin', cranked up and gettin' down. In New York City, for thirty-five dollars visitors can purchase the worship of African Americans along with tours of the Statue of Liberty, Wall Street, Times Square, and Central Park. These national and international visitors are loaded onto buses and head to Harlem for the Gospel Tour, where they attend churches with designated seating areas and are provided the best in African American church entertainment. They rarely stay for the sermon because the tour includes a soul-food meal at one of the local restaurants, and the reservations must be kept.

Entertainment or Worship

In some churches worship is at best entertainment. In *Tozer on Worship and Entertainment* the author warns:

> Pastors and churches in our hectic times are harassed by the temptation to seek size at any cost and to secure by inflation what they cannot gain by legitimate growth. The mixed multitude cries for quantity and will not forgive a minister who insists upon solid values and permanence. Many a man of God is being subjected to cruel pressure by the ill-taught members of his flock who scorn his slow methods and demand quick results and a popular following regardless of quality. These children play in the marketplaces and cannot overlook the affront we do them by our refusal to dance when they whistle or to weep when they out of caprice pipe a sad tune. They are greedy for thrills, and since they dare no longer seek them in the theater, they demand to have them brought into the church.[5]

It is a heresy when ministers and musicians refuse to plan worship. Musicians complain that they are not able to reach the pastor because he or she is busy, out of town, running revivals, or fulfilling speaking engagements, and therefore worship will have to get along as best it can. A successful worship service in many churches is measured by the fact that the pastor and the choir stirred up frenzy on Sunday morning and the people were glad. Whether or not the members of the congregation can recall the sermon title or text is not important as long as they got their shout on.

The idea of getting the people up has been misused, misinterpreted, and mishandled in many instances. Pastors will send musicians in to get the service up and running to prepare for their grand entrance and divine "word," sometimes even from the Lord. The truth is that everyone should begin and end worship together. Worship should begin with all of the participants in the liturgy in place. The concept of a grand late entrance is most associated with secular entertainment. There are the opening acts and then the main attraction. "For centuries," A. W. Tozer cautions us, "the Church stood solidly against every form of worldly entertainment, recognizing it for what it was—a device for wasting time, a refuge from the disturbing voice of conscience, a scheme to divert attention from moral accountability. For this she got herself abused roundly by the sons of the world. But of late she has become tired of the abuse and has given over the struggle. She appears to have decided that if she cannot conquer the great god Entertainment she may as well join forces with him and make whatever use she can of his powers. . . . The church that can't worship must be entertained. And men who can't lead a church to worship must provide the entertainment."[6]

So that we are not guilty of entertaining instead of worshiping, let's consider the major components of worship. Some worship traditions label these The Gathering, The Spoken Word of God, The Response to the Word of God, and The Sending and Going Forth. Webber suggests that worship unfolds in four parts: we prepare to worship, we hear God speak, we respond to God, and God sends us forth.[7] Eight principles for worship accompany his claim:

Worship Celebrates Christ
Worship Tells and Acts Out the Christ-Events
In Worship God Speaks and Acts
Worship Is an Act of Communication
In Worship We Respond to God and Each Other
Return Worship to the People
All Creation Joins in Worship
Worship As a Way of Life[8]

As one begins to plan worship he or she must first know what worship is. A variety of definitions have been offered. C. Welton Gaddy says, "Worship is a gift between lovers who keep on giving to each other."[9] A. S. Herbert describes worship as "the recognition and acknowledgement at every level of human nature of the absolute worth of God."[10] William Temple expands on that theme when he writes, "Worship is the submission of all our nature to God. It is the quickening of the conscience by His holiness; the nourishment of the mind with His truth; the purifying of imagination by His beauty; the opening of the heart to His love; the surrender of will to His purpose—and all of this gathered up in adoration, the most selfless emotion of which our nature is capable."[11]

Finally, in his book *The Integrity of Worship*, Paul W. Hoon maintains that "Christian worship is God's revelation of himself in Jesus Christ and man's response," or a twofold action: that of "God to the human soul in Jesus Christ and in man's responsive action through Jesus Christ."[12]

Effective Planning for Worship

In *African American Worship*, Talbot writes that "two contemporary management planners have defined planning as 'deciding in advance what to do, how to do it, when to do it and who is to do it.' The definition summarizes the essential elements in planning: what, how, when, and who. Planning bridges the gap from where we are to where we want to go. It makes it possible for things to occur which would not otherwise happen and although the best laid plans can fail to materialize, without some form of planning events are left to chance. Experience shows that nothing significant happens when left to chance."[13]

With a clear understanding of worship the minister and the musician then can begin to plan worship effectively. The church is not a religious theater where performers are paid to amuse those who attend. It is an assembly of redeemed sinners—men and women called unto Christ and commissioned to spread his gospel to the ends of the earth.[14] The temptation to provide entertainment will be defeated when this understanding is foremost in the planning.

Planning worship should not be sporadic, seasonal, unreliable, or for convenience. It must be consistent, regular, and reliable. There must be sufficient time for the musician to select and prepare the choir for special sermons, topics, or emphases. Worship planned in advance will allow both the minister and the musician to investigate, gather, and study relevant materials. To plan effectively, Costen suggests, we must

- Consider the lived experiences of worshipers and their understanding of worship.
- Consider the worship space.
- Become familiar with your denominational polity and theology of worship to determine what elements are required and what your denomination believes about each of the elements.
- Use Scripture to undergird the entire worship event.
- Consider the flow of the service to determine what patter facilitates worship in the particular congregation.
- Take care that the language of the liturgy is inclusive.[15]

The challenge in worship is to discover continual enjoyment and enthusiasm in an oft-repeated exercise. Finding new ways to present the old story should be the constant challenge and delight of the minister and the musician. If the Christian Year is not used in planning worship, it is good to center worship around a theme—a focal point or central idea that gives the service sequence and depth. Of course the sermon topic is a natural focal point.[16] The pastor, worship leader, and musician must communicate regularly about sermon topics. Once they have been established, worship resources and other materials can be selected and utilized more adequately.

Many times people come to church and feel like spectators instead of worshipers. They merely watch worship instead of worshiping. The best way to counter this spectatorism is to give the people ample opportunities to participate—through singing, reading, and praying—and by using members of the congregation in various parts of the service. "We seek variety," explains Howard Stevenson, "not for its own sake or because we want to put on a good show, but because we serve a God of infinite variety. We want to catch a glimpse of [God's] face and [God's] character from every possible angle. Each new revelation of truth and beauty, and every expression of love and concern, helps us understand [God] more. Worship is the ceaseless activity of heaven; one day, it will be our Eternal activity. The practice of worship here on earth is perhaps our most significant preparation for the life to come."[17]

To revitalize African American worship with "new eyes for seeing," as the subtitle of his book says, Talbot reminds us that

> Worship should be remembering.
> Worship should be theologically sound.
> Worship should be relevant to life now with all of its perils
> and promises.
> Worship should be inclusive of all God's people and enable
> their participation.
> Worship should result in developing a sense of mission.
> Worship should express itself in "generous" language.
> Worship should be sociological and seek to reorient life
> by answering the crucial question: "What happens after the
> Doxology has been sung and the Benediction has been
> pronounced?"[18]

Or, as Watley cautions, "We must be flexible in our worship and not
get so caught up and upset about what is on the printed bulletin."
He continues, "One Sunday at St. James the Spirit fell, and it
was obvious that it was preaching time. I called for the sermonic
hymn and took my text. After the service, one of my anal-retentive,
high-liturgical members came up to me and said, 'Reverend,
you forgot to acknowledge the visitors and call for Sister So-and
So who had a presentation to make to the Building Fund.' I told
her that I didn't forget but that when the Holy Ghost comes
everything changes. After that Sunday and until this very Sunday,
at the top of our bulletin is the heading: 'The worship is under
the direction of the Holy Spirit and subject to change without
notice.'"[19]

In black worship there is a sense of what James H. Cone calls
"the eschatological community." This is found in the belief that the
Spirit of Jesus is coming to visit the congregation in the worship,
or what Zan W. Holmes Jr., pastor of the St. Luke Community
United Methodist Church in Dallas, refers to as "encountering
Jesus in worship." He explains:

This presence of the Holy Spirit is a liberating experience from complete control of the ritual. Ritual is important, but it is not an end in itself. Ritual is interrupted freely when the Spirit moves. This clock is not worshiped. The preacher is told by the congregation, "Take your time!" And if he or she is saying something, the people will stay and listen, for part of what happens when the Spirit visits is a radical transformation in the people's identity. Those who were no people become God's people. Those who have thought of themselves as nobody become somebody. You can see it in their walk. You can hear it in their talk. And if you give them a chance, they will tell the story of how an encounter with Jesus enabled them to overcome their lack of identities![20]

I strongly recommend Holmes's *Encountering Jesus* for pastors, worship leaders, musicians, and laypersons. He concisely addresses encountering Jesus in the Bible, in worship, in preaching, in the life of the church and the community, and in seeking justice.[21]

It is essential to have a well-planned worship service, but when the Holy Spirit shows up, the worship is subject to change by the One whom we worship. We must never confuse pomp for praise or emotionalism for spirituality. "God is spirit, and his worshipers must worship in spirit and in truth" (John 4:24, NIV).

We must also be able to discern and distinguish worship from entertainment, spirituality from emotionalism, sanctified substance from self-constructed styles, prophetic proclamation from pleasing-to-everybody preaching, theological truth from tired traditions, Christian content from cultural ceremonies, relevant reason from repeated rituals, Christ-centered worship from self-centered agendas, and total praise from praise-team prompted cheerleading.

It must be the unswerving and nonnegotiable commitment of the pastor, the musician, and the worship leaders to adequately plan, pray, and implement worship so that Mt. Zion may rejoice in spirit and in truth!

CHAPTER SEVEN

HYMNODY IN THE CHURCH

HEN THE PSALMIST DAVID DECLARED, "O SING UNTO THE LORD a new song; for he hath done marvellous things: his right hand, and his holy arm, hath gotten him the victory" (Psalm 98:1, KJV), I am sure David could not have imagined a time when the people of God would have a limited hymnody to express their praise, adoration, and thanksgiving to God for all that he has done for them.

Congregational singing is to be a purposeful act in worship, never merely a way to fill time or a matter of routine. By means of corporately voiced songs, a call to worship can be sounded, praise can be declared, faith can be confessed, a text from the Bible can be heralded, repentance can be invited, a prayer can be offered, and sacrifice can be encouraged.[1] The church's worship is strengthened if congregational singing is utilized in service to all of these worshipful purposes.

Why We Sing Hymns

Hymns provide congregations opportunity to express their beliefs about faith and doctrine and their experiences of the Christian life. To be an authentic expression of faith, the beliefs embodied in the hymns must be true, based on Scripture, and in keeping with the accepted doctrines of the congregation. Hymns express doctrinal truths about God the Father and God's presence in the world; truths about Jesus Christ the Son and his work as Savior and Redeemer; and truths about the Holy Spirit, the Enabler and Comforter. These are theological expressions. Theology—the study and understanding of God—is a significant part of hymnology, the study and understanding of hymns.

In singing hymns, the singer experiences a greater awareness of God: God's character, attributes, and provisions for God's children.[2] Hymns at their most apparent level are text and tune, but because of their nature—human creation in response to the divine—they can evoke in us commitment, adoration, comfort, joy, faith, fellowship, and community. Hymns communicate to others what we are about and what we believe. They also communicate an affirmation of the divine and how we experience God in our lives and spiritual journey. Hymns take on the form of a dialogue within the community of worshipers as well as in our individual devotions and prayers to God.[3]

If we are to sing and pray (often we do both at the same time) with spirit and understanding, we must mean what we say and know what we mean. Unless the hymns we use in worship express our convictions, we might as well sing the stock-market reports, the real-estate ads from the daily newspaper, or a list of names from the telephone directory.[4]

Yet there is widespread evidence of church members' lack of attention to the ideas uttered in hymns. Few people will go so far as the organist who told me, "In hymn singing, words are important only to the extent that they stay out of the way of the music." But the practice of many leaders and congregations betrays an attitude disturbingly similar. Not all of the dissonance in church music is struck audibly by singers and accompanists. Many "discords" are produced by theological concepts out of harmony with Christian truth, by religious ideas contradictory to the experiences and beliefs of the worshipers, by unexamined spiritual clichés, or by fine-sounding words that lack any clear meaning.[5]

In a lecture J. Wendell Mapson Jr. declared that "congregational hymn singing is almost a lost art in the Black church. We allow the choir to do all of the singing with their special arrangements and contemporary songs that people may enjoy, but cannot participate in." He went on to remind us that

this spectator worship is not the kind of worship pleasing to
God. Congregational singing is in the intensive care unit
breathing its last breath. Let's go back to the hymns of our
faith, and sing them with life, and spirit, and joy. Lift the rafters
singing, "Come, Thou Fount of Every Blessing," "O for a
Thousand Tongues to Sing," "Jesus Is All the World to Me,"
"Since Jesus Came into My Heart," " My Faith Looks Up to
Thee," "More Love to Thee, O Christ."

If the choir cannot sing, won't sing or is too cute to sing,
sing anyhow.[6]

The secularization, commercialization, and industrialization of
gospel music in the United States since the early 1970s has reduced
congregational singing to accommodate additional choral selections from the Top Forties charts and local radio stations' most
requested hits. This reduction of congregational singing has
decreased worshipers' participation in communicative worship,
leaving them to become mere spectators. Congregations have
become audiences that applaud, react, and reinforce the choir and
the minister, who also too often are reduced to performers.

Recovering Lost Traditions

Since the 1950s, more music has been published for congregational singing than at any other time in the history of the church.
Nearly all the major denominational bodies, as well as many independent congregations and publishing companies, have produced
official and supplemental hymnals and related collections of songs.
In almost every case, these collections evidence a recovery of traditions once lost and relentless pursuit of contemporary music that is
both faithful to the gospel and representative of the languages, both
verbal and musical, of modern culture.

The influences of black theology and Afrocentrism in the
African American church have contributed to the increase of
African American hymnals published by various denominations,
and these new hymnals have replaced the hymnals of the dominant
society. In 1977 the National Baptist Publishing Board published
The New National Baptist Hymnal. In 1981 the United Methodist

Church published *Songs of Zion* and the Episcopal Church published *Lift Every Voice and Sing*. The first official hymnal of the Church of God in Christ, *Yes, Lord!* was published in 1982. In 1984 a revised edition of its 1954 hymnal was published by the African Methodist Episcopal Church; it was entitled *AMEC Bicentennial Hymnal*. In 1987 G.I.A. Publications, Inc. published *Lead Me, Guide Me*, and in 1993 the Episcopal Church published *Lift Every Voice and Sing II*. In 1999 the Evangelical Lutheran Church in America and the Lutheran Church—Missouri Synod published the hymnal *This Far by Faith*. Early in 2001, G.I.A. Publications released *The African American Heritage Hymnal* containing 580 hymns, 52 litanies for the black liturgical year, and 52 responsive readings. This is one of the most significant ecumenical hymnals ever created for African American churches.

With this plethora of hymnals available, it seems impossible that the hymnody of most mainline African American church congregations would consists of fewer than fifty hymns, including Christmas carols and Easter hymns. In some cases, it is fewer than twenty-five hymns, and in other cases, churches sing still fewer hymns and use no hymnal. Consider this list from a survey of choir directors, organists, choir librarians, ministers, and church secretaries from across the United States:

A Charge to Keep I Have
A Mighty Fortress Is Our God
Abide with Me, Fast Falls the Eventide
★All Hail the Power of Jesus' Name
   (Tunes: Diadem and Coronation)
All the Way My Savior Leads Me
Am I a Soldier of the Cross?
★Amazing Grace
Angels We Have Heard on High
★At the Cross
Beams of Heaven
★Blessed Assurance
Blessed Quietness

★Blest Be the Tie That Binds
Christ Arose!
Christ the Lord Is Risen Today
Come to Jesus
Come, Thou Almighty King
★Come Thou Fount of Every Blessing
Come, Ye Disconsolate
★Down at the Cross
Give Me a Clean Heart
★Go Tell It on the Mountain
God Be with You
★God of Our Fathers
★God Will Take Care of You
★Great Is Thy Faithfulness
Guide Me, O Thou Great Jehovah
Hark! the Herald Angels Sing
Have Thine Own Way, Lord!
He Lives
He Will Remember Me
★Higher Ground
★His Eye Is on the Sparrow
★Hold to God's Unchanging Hand
★Holy, Holy, Holy
How Firm a Foundation
How Great Thou Art
★I Am on the Battlefield for My Lord
I Am Thine, O Lord
I Heard the Voice of Jesus Say
I Love Thy Kingdom, Lord
★I Love to Tell the Story
I Must Tell Jesus
★I Need Thee Every Hour
I Surrender All
★I Will Trust in the Lord
If Jesus Goes with Me
★I'll Fly Away

*In the Garden
Is Your All on the Altar?
It Came Upon a Midnight Clear
*It Is Well with My Soul
Jesus Is All the World to Me
*Jesus, Keep Me Near the Cross
Jesus Paid It All
Jesus, Savior, Pilot Me
*Jesus, the Light of the World
*Joy to the World
*Just As I Am
Keep Me Every Day
*Lead Me, Guide Me
Lead Me to Calvary
Let All the People Praise Thee
*Lift Him Up
Love Divine, All Loves Excelling
*Love Lifted Me
More about Jesus
More Love to Thee, O Christ
*Must Jesus Bear the Cross Alone?
*My Faith Looks Up to Thee
My Heavenly Father Watches Over Me
*My Hope Is Built on Nothing Less (The Solid Rock)
My Jesus, I Love Thee
*Nearer My God to Thee
*Never Alone
No, Not One
Nothing But the Blood of Jesus
*O Come, All Ye Faithful
O for a Thousand Tongues to Sing
O God, Our Help in Ages Past
*O How I Love Jesus
*O I Want to See Him
O Little Town of Bethlehem
O Zion, Haste

On Jordan's Stormy Banks I Stand
Onward Christian Soldiers
*Pass Me Not, O Gentle Savior
Praise Him! Praise Him!
*Precious Lord, Take My Hand
Redeemed
Rejoice, Ye Pure in Heart
*Revive Us Again
Rock of Ages
Savior, More Than Life to Me
*Silent Night, Holy Night
Since Jesus Came into My Heart
Softly and Tenderly
Something Within Me
Stand by Me
Stand Up for Jesus
*Standing on the Promises
*Sweet Hour of Prayer
Sweet, Sweet Spirit
Take My Life and Let It Be
Take Your Burden to the Lord and Leave It There
The Blood Will Never Lose Its Power
*The Church's One Foundation
The Comforter Has Come
The First Noel
The Old Rugged Cross
The Unclouded Day
There Is a Fountain Filled with Blood
There Is Power in the Blood
Thou My Everlasting Portion (Close to Thee)
'Tis So Sweet to Trust in Jesus
*To God Be the Glory
Trust and Obey
*We'll Understand It Better By and By
*We're Marching to Zion
*We've Come This Far by Faith

★What a Fellowship
★What a Friend We Have in Jesus
When I Survey the Wondrous Cross
★When We All Get to Heaven
Where He Leads Me
★**Yes, God Is Real**
★Yes, Jesus Loves Me
★Yield Not to Temptation
★**You Can't Beat God Giving**

★ indicates the most frequently sung hymns
bold print indicates hymns by African American hymn writers

This list reflects only the hymns from those surveyed, but it far exceeds the hymns of many churches and cannot account for other hymns that our African American congregations sing regularly in worship services. This list does not represent the total hymnic vocabulary of other African American churches.

In *Somebody's Calling My Name*, Wyatt Tee Walker convincingly argues that "a survey of the musical content of the Black religious tradition can serve as an accurate commentary of what was happening to the Black community and its response to those conditions. Simply put, what Black people are singing religiously will provide a clue as to what is happening to them sociologically."[7] The body of hymnody in the mainline African American church is almost exclusively Euro-American, with the exception of a few hymns by Charles Albert Tindley, Lucie E. Campbell, Kenneth Morris, Andrae Crouch, Doris Akers, Margaret Douroux, E. C. Deas, and Thomas A. Dorsey.

These hymns have been preserved and perpetuated in the canon of the African American religious experience primarily because of their texts. The texts and music that accompanies them were relevant, applicable, conforming, righteous, and unimpeachable with their expressions of praise, adoration, honor, glory, struggle, hopes, joys, aspirations, faith, admonition, pilgrimage, and tribulations. "About one-half of the hymns listed have 'Jesus themes,' mirroring the centrality of Jesus in the Black religious experience," Walker notes in his analysis of these hymns. "Admittedly, the Jesus umbrella includes such topics as 'Trust and Confidence,' 'Cross and Resurrection,' 'Praise and Adoration,' but the fixation of the Black religious community on Jesus is widely known. . . . One-fourth of the hymns thematically expresses 'Dependence on God,' one-tenth 'Praise and Adoration' and one-tenth 'Death and Immortality.' The remaining five percent is divided among other religious themes."[8]

Wendell P. Whalum asserts that black Methodists and Baptists endorsed Isaac Watts's hymns, but the Baptists "blackened" them. They threw out the meter and rhythm and before 1875 had begun a new system that, although it was based on the style of singing coming from England to America in the eighteenth century, was drastically different from it.[9] J. Wendell Mapson Jr. adds, "The singing of hymns has always been a great experience in the black worship idiom, and often hymns sound differently when sung in black churches than when they are sung in white churches."[10]

Walker contributes this insightful observation:

> The Black religious community, increasingly urban, took the Euro-American hymn tunes and gave them an exaggerated measure, syncopation, and rendered them in the "surge" style closely akin to [the black] musical imprint on the meter music tradition. This "improvisation" was augmented by either the piano or organ, and after the turn of the century both. Once Black folks laid hands on the Euro-American hymns and gave them the musical overlay common to the Spiritual and the Black meter music tradition, the hymns would be forever changed. This fact is obvious when the original hymn tune is sung "straight," or precisely as the musical notation demands, and then is compared with a rendition by any random body of Black worshipers who have never seen one another before. The lyric texts are identical, but the performance, musically, is another kind altogether.[11]

While the previously listed hymns have been the most popular, most sung, and most loved among African American churches, the representation of hymns by African American hymn writers—

Tindley, Dorsey, Campbell, Morris, Willa Townsend and A. M. Townsend, B. B. McKinney, William Herbert Brewster Sr., Roberta Martin, Akers, Douroux, Deas, Crouch, James Cleveland, David Hurd, and many others—are very few. It is not that they do not exist. It is that the church has neither known them nor sung them. Eminent scholars, pastors, theologians, and musicians are now paying much needed attention to the African American Christian Year. This attention encourages the expansion, addition, and augmentation of hymnody in the African American church.

How Can We Evaluate Hymns?

As we expand our hymnody in the African American church, let us consider these guidelines from S. Paul Schilling for evaluating hymns:

Is it structurally sound? Does it have a central theme and organic unity of ideas?

Does it manifest progression of thought rather than repetitiveness or circularity?

Is it brief enough to be sung as a unit in worship?

Are its lines poetic, euphonious, and aesthetic; or trite, grating, and slipshod?

Are its words and phrases put together in orderly, connected fashion, or does it disregard generally accepted laws of grammar and syntax?

Do the accented syllables conform to a regular rhythm suitable for singing, and do the units of thought end with the ends of lines, avoiding "run-ons"? These conditions do not apply to poetry as such, but they do disqualify many poems of superior quality for use as hymns.

Is the language simple, concrete, and direct, using mainly words in common use; or stiff, archaic, ornate, or florid?

Does its verbiage balance the intellectual and the emotional, avoiding both dry abstraction and effusive sentimentality?

Does it say something clearly and coherently without being coldly and precisely propositional?[12]

In the preface to *The Hymn Book* of the Anglican Church of Canada and the United Church of Canada (1971), the editors state that the hymnal "must be Christian, an expression of faith in God as revealed in Christ, rather than an effusion of generalized religious sentiment. It must provide hymns, the quality of which must be that they are worthy of being offered to God in praise and reverence with integrity. It must be a vital vehicle of worship, not an anthology of Christian classics, but a well-balanced selection of hymns that will enable the congregation to offer praise appropriate to every service of worship and every season of the Christian Year."[13]

If we observe Schilling's guidelines for evaluating hymns, we should be able to ensure such worthiness from the standpoint of literary merit. However, songs that are to relate worshipers to God with integrity must heed standards of religious truth as well as those of good literature.

Since the Scriptures are the church's earliest witness to the creative, redemptive, renewing, and fulfilling activity of God in human life and history, they constitute our primary point of reference. With regard to any hymn, we therefore need to ask whether it is in harmony with the testimony of the biblical writings. This means not looking for proof texts but relating the basic message of a hymn to relevant biblical passages interpreted in the context of the Bible as a whole, in the light of enquiries of competent scholars, and with openness to the guidance of the Holy Spirit. Our hymnody is full of biblical language and imagery and informed by biblical faith. Therefore we shall want to ask how authentically a particular hymn reflects some facet of the truth contained in the Scriptures.[14]

If we are to adhere to the apostolic admonition to sing intelligently, to sing with understanding (1 Corinthians 14:15), we must use reason as one major criterion in hymn evaluation. Schilling explains that "we may need to rid ourselves of a frequent misunderstanding: reason does not entail a coldness. Barren one-sided intellectualism that stifles warmhearted feeling and subjects the rich fullness of human life to its autonomous, imperious authority. Reason is simply the thinking activity of the whole person which seeks to discover truth by criticizing, relating, ordering, and interpreting coherently the data of our conscious experience. Hence, when we examine a hymn from the perspective of reason we ask whether its assertions are internally consistent and whether they are connected harmoniously with one another and with other affirmations of Christian faith."[15]

Our hymnody must also reflect the African American religious experience and heritage. Walker asserts that "Afrocentric Christian theology proceeds from a different center than does traditional Euro-centric theology. The theology of African American Christians issues from our pain-predicament (which has been pervasive) and thereby, is more experiential than reflective. Ours is a learned and lived theology. This is not to suggest that the religious faith of African Americans is impervious to Continental musings but only that Afrocentricity is dominant." He continues,

> The sacred music of African Americans reveals the answers to the questions of any Christian theological inquiry:
>
> What is the view of God [or] (Jesus)?
> What is the view of humankind?
> What is the view of Judgment?
> What is the view of Salvation?
> What is the view of justice?
>
> Samples of music of the Afrocentric Christian Faith are (1) Bible-centered, (2) Jesus-centered, (3) Hope/Faith-centered, and (4) eschatos-centered.[16]

We can preserve and continue to sing a rather limited and select number of hymns in the African American church. But let us be challenged to use much more of the hymnal and to search the texts. We can learn the music accurately and improvise tastefully when that may be desired. We can also select hymns that will complement the Christian Year or the Christ events (Advent, Christmas, Epiphany, Lent, Holy Week, Easter, and Pentecost) and other themes and topics of the church. Better communication between the pastor and the musician will provide a much more meaningful and coherent worship experience of Word and song while it strengthens and enriches the congregation's singing in praise and worship to God.

How Hymns Influence Worship

The selection of hymns has a powerful influence on the overall mood and worship experience. Howard Stevenson once said, "The array of congregational songs is like a toolbox. Just as a builder selects a hammer to drive a nail and a screwdriver to set a screw, worship leaders must choose various songs from particular purposes."[17] When we become more intentional, prayerful, and selective about our hymns, the worship of God's people is enhanced, enriched, enlivened, and uplifted. When we make selections either at random or detached from the purpose of worship, we foster the disconnection of the worshiper from the most important reason for gathering in the Lord's house. It is the obligation of any director of music ministries to ensure that the music of worship begins with praise and adoration and ends with a blessing. Therefore the first hymns should praise God and proclaim broad themes that speak of unassailable truths, such as the power, sovereignty, immortality, and unchangeable and steadfast nature of God. The psalmist David exhorts us to "come before [God's] presence with thanksgiving, and make a joyful noise unto [God] with psalms" (Psalm 95:2, KJV). The worshipers should thereafter have opportunities through hymns to call upon God, to ask that God intercede on their behalf and others', to testify to God's activity in their lives, to invite nonbelievers to confess Christ, and to seek God's blessing until their next gathering. With inspired writers of God's Word, worshipers ought to be singers of the Word:

> The LORD bless you
> and keep you;
> the LORD make his face to shine upon you
> and be gracious to you;
> the LORD turn his face toward you
> and give you peace. (Numbers 6:24-26, NIV)

The vitality of the church and good hymn singing depend upon the mutual interaction of music and theology. "Music and theology are interrelated and interdependent," Robin A. Leaver reminds us. "The Bible is concerned with practical theology, the understanding and explanation of the interaction between God and [humankind], and also with practical music, the accompaniment to that interaction. Theology prevents music from becoming an end in itself by pointing us to its origins—in the doxology of creation. Music prevents theology from becoming a purely intellectual matter by moving [our] hearts to consider its ultimate purpose—the doxology of new creation."[18]

CHAPTER EIGHT

ANTHEMS IN THE CHURCH

I T IS THE FIRST OR THIRD SUNDAY IN A NONLITURGICAL African American church, and the Senior Choir no. 1, sometimes called the Chancel Choir, the Sanctuary Choir, the Senior Adult Choir, or the main church choir, occupies the choir loft. It is time for the morning anthem, and one can just about predict which one of eight or ten anthems the choir is about the sing. Although this may vary from church to church, the choir proudly proclaims that its repertoire consists only of anthems, arranged spirituals, hymns and hymn arrangements, and occasionally "light and refined" gospel. This singing organization will usually present the annual Christmas and/or Easter cantata, oratorios, pageants, and other extended works.

It is logical to associate the use of anthems in the African American church with the introduction of choral singing in the African Methodist churches. Whereas some Northern black ministers modified the structure of traditional Protestant services to meet the special cultural and religious needs of their congregations, others elected to structure their congregations around the doctrines, literature, and musical practices of white denominations.

Changes in Worship Style
One of the first major conflicts that divided members of independent black churches involved musical practices. Bishop Daniel Payne in the African Methodist Episcopal Church campaigned to change the style of worship that characterized this church. Influenced by his training at a Lutheran seminary and his tenure as

pastor in a Presbyterian church, Payne addressed what he perceived to be the problem of the AME Church. "The time is at hand when the minister of the A.M.E. Church must drive out this heathenish mode of worship or drive out all of the intelligence," he asserted. "Little active participation may make the worshiper nothing more than a spectator refinement, and practical Christians."[1] He opposed the singing of spirituals, which he referred to as "cornfield ditties." He also objected to the hand clapping, foot stamping, and "voodoo dances" that often accompanied the spirituals. Payne was committed to teaching and preaching "the right, fit, and proper way of serving God."[2]

Payne made his first change in the services of black Methodists by replacing the practice of lining out hymns (which he thought was primitive and unsophisticated) with choral singing and instrumental music.[3] These changes were instituted in Bethel Church in Philadelphia (1841-1842) and in Bethel Church in Baltimore (1848-1849). Many members responded to these so-called improvements by complaining, "You have brought the devil into the Church, and therefore we will go out." According to Payne, "When choirs were introduced in the church, many went out of Bethel, and never returned."[4]

The adoption of choral singing in many northern Methodist churches resulted in withdrawals and splits in congregations throughout the United States. In spite of controversy regarding his innovations, Payne defended the sweeping changes he had made: "The moral and religious effects of choral singing have been good, especially when the whole or a majority of the choir were earnest Christians. I have witnessed spiritual effects produced by Bethel choir in Philadelphia, and by Bethel choir in Baltimore, equal to the most unctuous sermons from the lips of the most eloquent and earnest preachers, so that Christians did rejoice as though they were listening to the heavenly choir which the shepherds heard on the plains of Bethlehem announcing the advent of the Savior."[5]

Although many people objected to Bishop Payne's "proper way of serving God" and his conservative philosophy of music in worship, black ministers in independent Presbyterian and Episcopal churches as well as Baptist churches shared his perspectives. (These churches exercised strict control over the order of worship and over the training of ministers as well.) One must agree with Payne, however, when he added, "A choir, with instruments as an accompaniment, can be made powerful and efficient auxiliary to the pulpit. Two things are essential to the saving power and efficiency of choral music—a scientific training and an earnest Christianity. Two things are necessary to make choral singing always profitable to a Church—that the congregation shall always join in the singing with the choir, and that they shall always sing with the spirit and the understanding."[6]

Writing about aspects of black worship, the Reverend Charles G. Adams notes:

> There is no other church where such a wide variety of music is integrated, rendered, and sustained within a unified experience of worship. . . . The anthem has a place in the worship service of most independent Black Methodist and Baptist congregations. The mastery of the anthem represents to the Black Choir the same kind of achievement as the rendering of German lieder represents to Roland Hayes and Marian Anderson. It is a sign of being progressive, liberated, and educated to be able to sing anthems, indicating a high level of technical musical attainment. The Christmas oratorio and the Easter cantata are annual events which along with the weekly rendering of a sacred anthem represent emancipation, education, and the freedom to understand and reflect the highest in white European and American musical culture. The worshippers who listen tolerantly to the anthems take just as much pride in being able to listen to them as do the singers in being able to perform them. Their presence in the worship service is an indication of a liberated congregation that has "arrived." Sometimes the communal contemplation of a familiar Biblical text of an anthem plus the pride and joy at having "arrived" intensifies into shouting on the anthem in certain churches known to be spiritually and emotionally uninhibited. Cornerstone Baptist Church in Brooklyn is known to shout aloud and demonstrate boisterously at the conclusion of a rousing anthem whose text is Psalm 150.[7]

In the liturgical churches—Catholic, Lutheran, and Episcopal— anthems are selected primarily to complement, support, and reinforce the season of the Christian Year from the prescribed Scripture readings of the day. In most nonliturgical African American churches the anthem functions quite differently. The nonliturgical African American churches—Baptist, Methodist, United Church of Christ, Disciples of Christ, Presbyterians, Church of God in Christ, Seventh Day Adventists, and others— observe Christmas, Palm Sunday, Good Friday, Easter (Resurrection Sunday), and more recently, Pentecost.

For nonliturgical African American churches, however, the major celebrations include the pastor's anniversary, the choirs' anniversaries, the ushers' anniversary, and the church anniversary. Added to these are Men's Day, Women's Day, Youth Day, Installation of Officers Sunday, Missionaries' Sunday, Deacons' Sunday, Mothers' Board Sunday, the Willing Workers' Anniversary, Ladies' Aid Society Sunday, Stewardship Sunday, Busy Bee Circle Sunday, Ten-Friend Pew Rally Sunday, Married Ministry Sunday, Singles' Ministry Sunday, and Black History Sunday or Month. On these occasions the anthem is usually one that the director or musician knows, likes, and can play. It may be what the choir likes, what is most requested from friends of the choir, or what pleases the congregation. Or the criterion may be what is up-tempo, what sounds dramatic and operatic, what has a loud and harmonically full ending, or what will feature the resident divas or divos. Most often, it is what can be sung well with the time constraints of two or three rehearsals for volunteer members.

A Limited Repertoire

These factors and others have lead to an unusually limited repertoire of anthems in the nonliturgical African American church. Between 1994 and 1998, choir directors, musicians, choir members, and pastors from various denominations throughout the United States were surveyed about the anthems used in their churches. Consider this list, which was compiled from that survey:

Western European

★Gloria in Excelsis (Glorious Is Thy Name)	Mozart
★Hallelujah Chorus (from *Messiah*)	Handel
★I Will Give Thanks unto Thee, O Lord	Rossini
★Sanctus (Holy, Holy)	Gounod
Great and Marvelous Are Thy Works	A. R. Gaul
Hallelujah (Psalm 150)	Lowendoski
Hallelujah! (from *The Mount of Olives*)	Beethoven
He Watching Over Israel	Mendelssohn
How Lovely Is Thy Dwelling Place	Brahms
I Waited for the Lord	Mendelssohn
★Inflammatus (When Thou Comest)	Rossini
Jesu, Joy of Man's Desiring	J. S. Bach
O Lord, Most Holy	Franck
Praise the Lord, O Jerusalem	Maunder
Praise Ye the Lord (Psalm 150)	Franck
Praise Ye the Lord	Randegger
Thanks Be to Thee	Handel
The Heavens Are Telling	Beethoven
The Heavens Are Telling	Haydn
The Omnipotence	Schubert

American

★Let Mount Zion Rejoice	J. B. Herbert
★Lift Up Your Heads, O Ye Gates	E. L. Ashford
★The Lord Is My Light	Frances Allitsen
★When I Survey the Wondrous Cross	Gilbert Martin
Alleluia	Randall Thompson
Almighty God of Our Fathers	Will James
Every Valley	John Ness Beck
Glorious Everlasting	Thomas Cousins
Ho! Everyone That Thirsteth	Will C. Macfarlane
Now Let Us All Praise God and Sing	Gordon Young
Now Sing We Joyfully Unto God	Gordon Young
Seek Ye the Lord	Roberts

The Battle Hymn of the Republic

arr. Ringwald and
Wilhousky

The Beatitudes

H. R. Evans

The Ten Commandments

Ringwald

With a Voice of Singing

Martin Shaw

African American

★Lift Every Voice and Sing

arr. Roland Carter

★Listen to the Lambs

R. Nathaniel Dett

I'll Never Turn Back No More

R. Nathaniel Dett

Let the People Sing Praise

Lena J. McLin

Magnify the Lord

Virginia DeWitty

My Soul Doth Magnify the Lord

Noah F. Ryder

Listed here are some of the most frequently performed extended works (oratorios and cantatas) that have become the warhorses of the nonliturgical African American church:

★*Messiah*   Handel
★*The Crucifixion*   Stainer
·★*The Seven Last Words of Christ*   Dubois
Elijah   Mendelssohn
Gloria   Vivaldi
Mass in G   Schubert
Olivet to Calvary   Maunder
Requiem   Brahms, Mozart,
                                        and Faure
The Creation   Haydn
The Holy City   A. R. Gaul

★ indicates the most frequently listed and sung

I must hasten to add that this list does not reflect the repertoire of every nonliturgical African American church choir, but it does reflect those most frequently mentioned by respondents nation-wide. And there is regional variety in anthem repertoire. For example, some anthems are sung more frequently in Philadelphia, Baltimore, and New York than they are in Atlanta, Birmingham, Chicago, Detroit, or Los Angeles. Many African American churches in Philadelphia and Baltimore have become renowned for having always performed and preserved some of the most marvelous anthems and church music ever heard. I will not dare attempt to mention names, but there are some outstanding nonliturgical African American church choirs and directors across the country that regularly perpetuate variety, contemporary literature, and consistent excellence in their anthem repertoire and total church music ministry.

The church choir director is faced with the challenge of keeping abreast of the trends and changes in church music. William B. Garcia addressed this when he stated, "More than ever before, [the church choir conductor] is looking to the black composer for both the revolutionary and the traditional in church choir literature. And rightly so, for the black composer's output includes some of both."[8]

It is both interesting and unfortunate that anthems by African American composers are so underrepresented in the preceding lists. With the exception of Dett, DeWitty, Carter, and Marvin Curtis (his anthems are not listed), the majority of the composers are European, Anglo-American, or Euro-American. I urge choir directors, pastors, and choir members to insist on singing anthems by African American composers. Among these composers are Adolphus Hailstork, Lena McLin, Marvin Curtis, Robert A. Harris, Julius Williams, Samuel Coleridge-Taylor, R. Nathaniel Dett, Wendell P. Whalum, Roland Carter, Nathan Carter, Uzee Brown, Glenn Burleigh, Lucie E. Campbell, Willis Lawrence James, Philip McIntyre, Eugene Hancock, Ulysses S. Kay, Mark Fax, Charles Coleman, Thomas Kerr Jr., Undine Smith Moore, Clarence Joseph Rivers, David Hurd, Edward H. Margetson, Don Lee White, and Willis Barnett. The works of these composers are recommended not merely because they were written by African Americans but because of the rich musical quality of the compositions. If a special occasion or season is approaching, a congregation might commission an anthem by any one of our fine, capable African American composers. It is a joyful and marvelous experience to sing a composition that a celebrated and competent African American composer wrote with you and your choir in mind. Professor Evelyn Davidson White's *Choral Music by African-American Composers*[9] remains the most authoritative and concise reference for these works to date.

Testing the Standards, Expanding the Repertoire

I would argue that at least three factors have contributed to the use of these warhorse anthems in the nonliturgical African American churches. First, these anthems have been successfully tested and tried by the African American religious experience. I call it the *text test*. The texts of these compositions are relevant, consistent, and meaningful in the worship of African Americans. They have underscored, reaffirmed, and reinforced biblical teachings, theological foundations, history, hope, liberation, faith, praise and worship, struggles for peace and justice, grace, mercy, and the eschatological. These anthems have musically interpreted the Word of God, and they have taught the doctrines related to the African American Christian experience.

Adams accurately accounts for the communal contemplation and reflection on familiar biblical texts that these anthems provide. Psalm 150 ("Praise Ye the Lord"), is perhaps the best known. Others include Psalm 23 ("The Lord Is My Shepherd"), Psalm 27 ("The Lord Is My Light"), Psalm 24:7-10 ("Lift Up Your Heads, O Ye Gates"), Psalm 48:1-2 ("Let Mount Zion Rejoice"), Psalm 84:1,2,4 ("How Lovely [Amiable] Is Thy Dwelling Place"), Psalm 137 ("By the Rivers of Babylon"), Isaiah 55:1-3 ("Ho, Everyone That Thirsteth"), Isaiah 55:6,7 ("Seek Ye the Lord"), and Revelation 19:6; 11:15; 19:16 ("Hallelujah Chorus").

Second, these anthems contain the musical characteristics of grandeur, power, beauty, dignity, elevation, magnificence, majesty, might, pomp, reflection, splendor, and transcendence that move the emotions and the heart and that please the ears of listeners as well as performers. The melodic, harmonic, rhythmic, and dynamic elements of these anthems coupled with the text have resulted in approval and acceptance from many African American churches. The music must be expressively powerful, give or take intellectualism, in order to be deeply moving.

"Difficult" and "intellectual" are not always synonymous with what one may call great music. If we are not careful, we can recklessly assume that intellectual depth is overwhelmingly important and what it takes to make a great anthem. There is intellectually profound music, music that is structurally complex, carefully worked out, full of integrated detail, and organized into a significant architectural whole. In Western culture, this kind of profundity is found almost exclusively in classical music—not all of it, but a lot of it.[10] The ultimate message, the ultimate force of any music lies in cumulative expressiveness. In other words, profundity may be of two kinds: that which is profound by virtue of its deep intellectual process coupled with expressiveness, and that which probes and ponders almost exclusively because of its expressiveness.

Finally, these anthems, like many of the hymns and spirituals of the African American church, have been sung down from generation to generation and have been placed in the musical canon or standard anthem repertoire of the African American religious experience by our forebears. Such anthems have become classics because they have withstood the test of time through many performances. They have a unique and personal relevance in the Christian worship and discipleship of the performers and the listeners. They have been and are accessible to, as well as performable by, African American church musicians and choirs and have become a part of the churches' history and most requested choral selections. There are many references to these anthems in sermons, testimonies, and writings in the African American church. If anthems are performed, it is the expectation that the choir will sing Rossini's "I Will Give Thanks Unto Thee, O Lord" for the pastor's or the church's anniversary and Thanksgiving. It is the expectation that the choir will sing Herbert's "Let Mount Zion Rejoice" for the church anniversary and many special occasions. It is the expectation that the choir will sing Ashford's "Lift Up Your Heads, O Ye Gates" or Faure's "The Palms" on Palm Sunday, and Dubois's

Seven Last Words of Christ on Good Friday. It is the expectation that the choir will perform the Christmas portion of Handel's *Messiah* before Christmas Day. It is the expectation, the tradition, almost the rule that certain anthems be sung on certain occasions or else . . .

The Danish philosopher Søren Kierkegaard once observed that many people conceive of worship as a dramatic production in which God is the prompter, the worship leaders (minister and choir) are the performers, and the people are the audience. But Kierkegaard insisted that worshipers are the performers, the worship leaders are the prompters, and God is the audience. I concur with Kierkegaard's assessment, if worship is ever to become what God intended it to be.

Just as gospel music, praise and worship songs, jazz masses, and Christian hip hop and liturgical dance are often unjustly labeled entertainment, so anthems can equally become or serve as entertaining and artistic masterpieces, unless the hearts of those who render them and the purpose and function for their use in worship are Christ-centered and worship-centered. As we sing the great anthems of the church, Bishop Payne's challenge with reference to 1 Corinthians 14:15 is worthy of our consideration: "always sing with the spirit, and sing with the understanding also."[11] The role of the choir in worship is to sing to the congregation, for the congregation, and with the congregation so that they may ultimately encounter God, the true audience to whom all praise, honor, and glory are due.

African American church choirs, states Adams, "are able to sing European music with the same fire, zeal, and conviction that they have received from their primary baptism into gospel music's spontaneity and creativity. Likewise, they are able to sing gospel music with the selfsame precision . . . they have learned from . . . European music. . . . The rationality of European music is sanctified and beautified by the startling spontaneity of African and African American artistic ingenuity and fervor." But, he emphasizes,

> The aim of all church choirs is to sing with the intensity of conviction that can move the souls of people who feel jaded,

empty, and defeated by the deadening oppressions, dynamics, and confusions of post modern culture. Even the strictest of music can be made spiritually dynamic and convincing if it is sung with enthusiasm and ecstasy. On the other hand, conviction that is not informed and enthusiasm that is not controlled will not be edifying. Undisciplined enthusiasm repels rather than attracts. Uncontrolled light blinds rather than illumines.[12]

The warhorse anthems of the nonliturgical African American church should continue to be sung and preserved with accuracy, power, precision, spirit, and understanding. They are a part of the musical definition of the African American religious experience. However, the repertoire needs to expand and further develop to reflect who we are now and how we have come to better know and serve God. Choirs must be faithful to observe Paul's instruction and mandate in Colossians 3:16-17, when he said, "Let the word of Christ dwell in you richly; teach and admonish one another in all wisdom; and with gratitude in your hearts sing psalms, hymns, and spiritual songs to God. And whatever you do, in word or deed, do everything in the name of the Lord Jesus, giving thanks to God the Father through him" (NRSV).

We must not allow prejudice, incompetence, lack of musical skills, ability, or understanding, and high-voltage emotionalism to discourage, divert, or dispose of the singing of anthems or psalms to honor, please, and glorify God! The negative and contradictory labels "music of the oppressor," "white folks' music," "elite and educated music," and "Eurocentric music" imply irrelevance to African Americans' experiences, struggles, and liberation. Those labels, which assume that all African Americans have the same experiences and that the African American church is monolithic, perpetrate a blatant misrepresentation of God's Word. "It is possible for oppressors to sing the music of the oppressed and be liberated."[13] And the oppressed have historically appropriated the music and texts of the oppressor for liberating purposes. How can one ignore the biblically based, theologically sound text of the anthem? African Americans who in legitimate anger at white oppression have mistakenly sought to impose gospel music set in motion a new round of bondage for themselves and others.[14]

Too often, what we don't know, we resist, resent, and protest. Thus some people who are unacquainted with or new to the reading of music are among those who oppose and resist anthems. Others who believe the genre can no longer speak to the changing congregation call for the elimination of the anthems from worship. I am persuaded, however, that the pastor, minister of music, and choirs can so lift up the biblical and personal relevance of an anthem's text that the hearts and minds of the congregation may be won to Christ even when it is unaccustomed to the anthem form. I have consistently observed that much opposition and resistance to anthems in the African American church are voiced and perpetuated by those whose training and skills or lack thereof have rendered them unable to perform those anthems. This resistance is usually a means to cover and defend the inability of musicians to teach, perform, or understand them. This is often the case for spirituals as well.

One week before his death Whalum passionately declared, "I hope to see the day that gospel choirs and senior choirs are disbanded in the black church, and that one seriously committed, well-balanced church choir would be formed and sing all of the music of the black sacred experience, and that with quality. One should not have to wait until the first Sunday to hear an anthem or the third or fourth Sunday to hear a gospel."[15] When we do this, we honor the apostle Paul's mandate in Colossians 3:16-17.

Adams's charge most appropriately summarizes the ultimate intent for the church choir: "Sing on, choir! Sing until the emptiness of materialistic cravings are filled with the transformative challenges of transcendent truth. Sing until dead hopes are revived, dead souls are resurrected and dead values emerge from the cold tombs of expedient compromise. Sing until people are persuaded to love and young minds are drawn to Christ. Sing until the preacher can preach and the church gets right. Sing until the power of the Lord comes down!"[16]

CHAPTER NINE

THE SPIRITUAL AS CONGREGATIONAL MUSIC

S THE ENSLAVED IN THE UNITED STATES HEARD SERMONS by the slave preacher that were based upon the Bible, they created songs in response. These songs, which we call spirituals, are records of a people who found the status, faith, values, order, and harmony they needed to survive by internally creating an expanded universe and spiritual freedom. They literally willed themselves reborn.

In *Deep River* and *The Negro Spiritual Speaks of Life and Death*, Howard Thurman has observed that within the Negro spiritual "is the secret of [the enslaved's] ascendency over circumstances and the basis of their assurances concerning life and death."[1] In spirituals, an oppressed African people suggested alternative theories of time. This is a profound insight of not only Thurman but also Miles Mark Fisher in *Negro Slave Songs in the United States*, John Lovell Jr. in *Black Song*, and Lawrence W. Levine in *Black Culture and Black Consciousness*. Building upon the work of earlier African American scholars and analyzing the spirituals, Levine has persuasively argued that a sense of sacred time operated, in which the present was extended backwards so that the characters, scenes, and events of the Old and New Testaments became dramatically alive and present.[2] In *Folk Songs of the American Negro*, John W. Work II asserts that African American songs are "full of Scripture, quoted and implied," because for centuries—if reading was permitted at all—the Bible was usually the only book the enslaved were allowed to "study."[3]

The early black church never had or needed a choir. The entire congregation sang. If a member of the congregation could not sing, he or she could pat a foot. If one could not pat a foot, one could clap hands. If people could not clap their hands, they could sway their heads. If they could not sway their heads, they could wave their hands. And if they could not do this, they could testify. Everyone was expected to participate, and they did. In many of our churches today, the spirituals that one may hear are anthemized and arranged spirituals for choir. Congregations rarely sing spirituals.

Defining the Spirituals

Fisher defines spirituals as "the utterances of an individual about an experience that had universal application . . . which incorporate religious terminology."[4] Lovell defines the Afro-American spiritual as "an independent folk song, born of the union of African tradition and American socio-religious elements. It was affected to a limited extent by the American Christian evangelical tradition and Anglo-American hymn, but not . . . the so called white spiritual."[5] A broad yet somewhat precise definition of spirituals for our purpose is that it is a type of sacred folk song created by an individual or individuals of a particular group and adopted by that group for singing. These songs may express emotions, religious or secular experiences, or attitudes. In churches that still sing spirituals, they are most commonly used in midweek prayer meetings and Sunday morning devotional services. They are not being sung down through oral transmission, which has kept them alive until this time. The spiritual as congregational music has been replaced by a few repetitive hymns, congregational songs of praise and worship, gospel music, and an abundance of choral selections.

When I was a student at Morehouse College, my professor, the late Wendell P. Whalum, admired John W. Work, R. Nathaniel Dett, James Weldon Johnson, Hall Johnson, Willis Lawrence James, and others for their work in preserving the Negro spiritual. I recall Dr. Whalum's unswerving commitment to the preservation of Negro folk songs, and he took advantage of every opportunity to hear them, sing them, and teach, arrange, and record them for the Glee Club and church choirs. He was the morning song leader for the Hampton Ministers' Conference for many years and used that time to revive and reinvigorate the spiritual. Ogden Hall provided the perfect acoustic setting as more than fifteen hundred conference participants enthusiastically sang as he led them from the podium. (See the Appendix for an example of his method.)

In Whalum's unparalleled article, "Black Hymnody," he affirmed that "the serious sacred music of the oral tradition is primarily individual-to-group music. It begins with the individual but is made into final composition, finished, and polished by the group. . . . Everyone is a participant. An individual contributed a musical 'thought,' and the group worked it over and over, reshaping phrases, adding and subtracting notes, filling in melodic gaps, adjusting harmony and rhythm. Many spirituals died when they failed to do what the group intended them to do."[6]

Zora Neale Hurston provides support for Whalum's claim in *The Sanctified Church.* She clearly differentiates and distinguishes between genuine spirituals and what she refers to as neo-spirituals:

> The real spirituals are not really just songs. They are unceasing variations around a theme. . . . There never has been a presentation of a genuine Negro spiritual to any audience anywhere. What is being sung by the concert artists and glee clubs are the works of Negro composers or adaptors *based* on the spirituals. Under this head come the works of Harry T. Burleigh, Rosamond Johnson, Lawrence Brown, Nathaniel Dett, Hall Johnson and [John W.] Work. All good work and beautiful, but *not* the spirituals. These neo-spirituals are the outgrowth of the glee clubs. Fisk University boasts perhaps the oldest and certainly the most famous of these. They have spread their interpretation over America and Europe. Hampton and Tuskegee have not been unheard.
>
> But with all the glee clubs and soloists, there has not been one genuine spiritual presented.
>
> To begin with, Negro spirituals are not solo or quartette material. The jagged harmony is what makes it, and it ceases to be what it was when this is absent. Neither can any group be trained to produce it. Its truth dies under training like flowers under hot water. The harmony of the true spiritual is not regular. The dissonances are important and not to be ironed out by the trained musician. The various parts break in at any

old time. Falsetto often takes the place of regular voices for short periods. Keys change. Moreover, each singing of the piece is a new creation. The congregation is bound by no rules. No two times singing is alike so, that we must consider the rendition of a song not a final thing, but as a mood. It won't be the same thing next Sunday.

Negro songs to be heard truly must be sung by a group, and a group bent on expression of feelings and not on sound effects.

Glee clubs and concert singers put on their tuxedos, bow prettily to the audience, get the pitch and burst into magnificent song—but not Negro song. The real Negro singer cares nothing about pitch. The first notes just burst out and the rest of the church join in—fired by the same inner urge. Every man trying to express himself through song. Every man for himself. Hence, the harmony and disharmony, the shifting of keys and broken time that make up the spiritual.[7]

It is important that I reiterate the purpose of this chapter by distinguishing the difference between the arranged spirituals to be sung by choirs (e.g., arrangements by Hall Johnson, William Dawson, Undine Smith Moore, Noah F. Ryder, Roland Carter, Moses Hogan, Andre Thomas, Brazeal Dennard, and others) and congregational spirituals that require a leader and a congregation to sing them, as Whalum and Hurston have illustrated. The latter have been neglected and forgotten in worship services of African American churches. By no means do I call for choirs to discontinue their renditions of the arranged concert spirituals as special choral offerings. In fact, choirs should always be encouraged to sustain and include the masterworks of the aforementioned composers and arrangers that are appropriate for worship.

Finding Collections of Spirituals

Some wonderful collections of spirituals for use as congregational music are still in print and available for purchase. Dover Publications in New York has recently reprinted *American Negro Songs and Spirituals* by John W. Work. *Religious Folk-Songs of the Negro*, edited by R. Nathaniel Dett, is available through the Hampton University Bookstore in Hampton, Virginia. In this collection,

which indexes the songs by subject, Dett refers to the spirituals
as hymns:

> That it was an error, centuries ago, on the part of the church
> to divorce religious music from rhythmic utterances, no one
> will now deny; even so, the most popular hymns ever have
> been those with a more or less pronounced rhythm. The
> Negro spiritual, combining as it does religious feeling with a
> regular, almost irresistible beat, based on a scale in existence
> five hundred years before Christ, having its own simple
> harmonies and archaic cadences, presents in an elemental form
> the solution of one of the great problems of Christianity; how
> to evolve a style of music that will convey a religious message
> through a popular medium without at the same time suggest-
> ing the things of the world.
>
> In such a volume as this, there is an opportunity, not only of
> experiencing the original psalms of suffering as born in the
> Negro breast, but also a greater opportunity of touching, as it
> were, the fringes of the robes of Grandeur, whose garments
> trail the dust but whose face, uplifted above the clouds, we are
> not yet permitted to see.[8]

Spirituals Triumphant, edited by Edward Boatner and Willa A.
Townsend and published by the Sunday School Publishing Board
of the National Baptist Convention, USA, in 1927, is one of the
most neglected and overlooked sources of spirituals for congregations. It is available through the Sunday School Publishing Board of
the National Baptist Convention, USA, Inc., in Nashville,
Tennessee. In the foreword A. M. Townsend writes, "With a large
number of spirituals in circulation, there is a tendency to get away
from the harmony and characteristic way in which these songs
were originally sung, and therefore, much of their real importance
is lost. To the end that the 'old-time' way of singing these songs may
be preserved, is this edition brought forth by the Sunday School
Publishing Board. No one can sing or write these songs of sorrow,
joy, hope, and fear, so nearly as they can be reproduced, as those
from whom the songs were originated."[9]

Additionally, *Spirits That Dwell in Deep Woods*, compiled and edited by Wyatt Tee Walker in three volumes, is an extraordinary recent collection of spirituals. These musical jewels were collected by Walker and musically notated and arranged by C. Eugene Cooper from the memory banks of past and present members of the Silver Strands, a senior adult choir of the Canaan Baptist Church of Harlem, New York. For each spiritual Walker provides an insightful introduction, biblical basis, theological mooring, lyric and form analysis, and contemporary commentary and exegesis.

It is interesting to note the number and variety of spirituals that appear in mainline denominational hymnals of the African American church. These include *The New National Baptist Hymnal* of the National Baptist Convention, USA; the *AMEC Bicentennial Hymnal* of the African Methodist Episcopal Church; and *Yes Lord!* the hymnal of the Church of God in Christ; along with *The Gospel Pearls*, published by the Sunday School Publishing Board of the National Baptist Convention, USA; and *Songs of Zion*, published by the United Methodist Publishing House and Abingdon Press.

The Gospel Pearls (1921)
Balm in Gilead
Going to Shout All Over God's Heaven
Great Day
I Couldn't Hear Nobody Pray
I Know the Lord's Laid His Hands on Me
I Will Pray (Ev'rytime I Feel the Spirit)
Inching Along
Lord, I Want to Be a Christian
Old Time Religion
Shine for Jesus (Jubilee—E. C. Deas and Julian Alford)
Somebody's Knocking at Your Door
Stand by Me (Charles A. Tindley)
Steal Away to Jesus
Surely He Died on Calvary
Swing Low
Wade in the Water
We Shall Walk Through the Valley

Were You There?
Witness for My Lord
You Won't Find a Man Like Jesus

The New National Baptist Hymnal (1977)
Amen!
Deep River
Don't Stay Away
Go Down, Moses
Go, Tell It on the Mountain
Great Day! Great Day!
He Arose
Hear Me Praying
I'm Gonna Sing
Kum Ba Yah
Let Us Break Bread Together
Lord, I Want to Be a Christian
My Lord, What a Morning
Oh, Freedom
Old Ship of Zion
Old Time Religion
On My Journey Home
Over My Head
Rise Up, Shepherd
Some O' These Days
Somebody's Knocking at Your Door
Soon-a Will be Done
Stand by Me (Charles Albert Tindley)
Standin' in the Need of Prayer
Steal Away to Jesus
Surely He Died On Calvary
Swing Low
This Little Light of Mine
Wade in the Water
Walk with Me
We Are Climbing Jacob's Ladder

We Shall Overcome
We Shall Walk Through the Valley in Peace
Were You There?

Songs of Zion (1981)
Ain't Dat Good News?
Amen (Traditional)
Balm in Gilead
Bye and Bye
Calvary
Certainly, Lord
Changed Mah Name
City Called Heaven
Climbin' Up d' Mountain
Come Out de Wilderness
De Gospel Train
De Ol' Ark's a-Moverin'
Deep River
Didn't My Lord Deliver Daniel?
Do, Lord, Remember Me
Ev'ry Time I Feel the Spirit
Ezek'el Saw de Wheel
Fix Me, Jesus
Free at Last
Freedom Train a-Comin'
Give Me Jesus
Glory, Glory Hallelujah
Go Down, Moses (Traditional)
Go, Tell It on the Mountain
God Is a God
Good News
Great Day
Hard Trials
He Arose
He Nevuh Said a Mumbalin' Word
He's Got the Whole World in His Hands

His Name So Sweet
Hold On
Hush, Hush, Somebody's Callin' My Name
I Been in de Storm So Long
I Couldn't Hear Nobody Pray
I Feel Like My Time Ain't Long
I Know the Lord's Laid His Hands on Me
I Stood on de Ribber ob Jerdon
I Want Jesus to Walk with Me
I Want to Be Ready
I'm a Rolling
I'm Gonna Sing
I've Been Buked
I've Got a Robe
Joshua Fit de Battle of Jericho
Jubilee
Keep a-Inchin' Along
King Jesus Is a Listenin'
Kum Ba Yah, My Lord
Let Us Break Bread Together
Little David, Play on Your Harp
Live a-Humble
Lord, I Want to Be a Christian
Mah God Is So High
Many Thousand Gone
Mary and Martha
My Good Lord's Done Been Here
My Lord! What a Morning
My Soul's Been Anchored in de Lord
No Hidin' Place
Nobody Knows the Trouble I See
Noboby Knows the Trouble I See, Lord
Oh, Freedom
Oh, Mary, Don't You Weep, Don't You Mourn
Oh! What a Beautiful City

Ole-Time Religion
On Ma Journey
Over My Head
Peer, Go Ring Them Bells
Plenty Good Room
Ride On, King Jesus
Rise an' Shine
Rockin' Jerusalem
Roll, Jordan, Roll
Scandalize' My Name
Sit Down, Servant, Sit Down
Somebody's Knocking at Your Door
Sometimes I Feel Like a Moanin' Dove
Sometimes I Feel Like a Motherless Chile
Soon-a Will be Done
Standin' in the Need of Prayer
Steal Away
Study War No More
Swing Low, Sweet Chariot
The Time for Praying
There's a Great Camp Meeting
There's a Meeting Here Tonight
This Little Light of Mine
'Tis the Old Ship of Zion
Trampin'
Tryin' to Get Home
Wade in the Water
We Shall Overcome
Were You There?
Woke Up Dis Mornin'
You Hear the Lambs a-Cryin'
You'd Better Min'

Yes Lord! (1982)
Ain't-a that Good News?

Come Out the Wilderness
Do Lord, Remember Me
Every Time I Feel the Spirit
Ezekiel Saw the Wheel
Good News! The Chariot's Coming
Have You Got Good Religion?
He Is King of Kings
He Never Said a Mumbling Word
I Shall Not Be Moved
I Will Trust in the Lord
I've Just Come from the Fount (His Name So Sweet)
O, Freedom
Rise Up, Shepherd
Some O' These Days
Standin' in the Need of Prayer
Swing Low, Sweet Chariot
Take Me to the Water
There Is a Balm in Gilead
'Tis the Old Ship of Zion
Woke Up This Morning
Yes, He Did!
You'd Better Mind

AMEC Bicentennial Hymnal (1984)
Amen, Amen
Dere's a Star in de East (Rise Up, Shepherd)
Go, Tell It on the Mountain
Great Day
Guide My Feet
I Couldn't Hear Nobody Pray
I Got a New Name
I Know I've Been Changed (The Angels in Heaven)
I Know the Lord's Laid His Hands on Me
I Want Jesus to Walk with Me
I'll Be Alright

I'm Gonna Live So God Can Use Me
Let Us Break Bread Together
Lord, I Want to Be a Christian
Lord, Make Me More Holy
My Lord, What a Morning
O the Rocks and the Mountains
See Four and Twenty Elders
Steal Away to Jesus
Sweet Jesus
Swing Low, Sweet Chariot
There Is a Balm in Gilead
They Crucified My Savior (He Arose)
We Are Climbing Jacob's Ladder
We Are Walking in the Light
Were You There?

These five collections represent an increase in the number of spirituals that can be found in the hymnals of African American congregations and set the stage for future publications. The magnificent and voluminous representation of spirituals in *Songs of Zion*, compiled and edited by William B. McCain, set the standard for other denominations and has influenced the inclusion of more sacred music by African Americans in their compilations. The Episcopal Church did so by publishing *Lift Every Voice and Sing* in 1981 and *Lift Every Voice and Sing II* in 1993. The Roman Catholic Church followed in 1987 with *Lead Me, Guide Me*, and in 1999, the Lutheran Church published *This Far by Faith*. Now we must sing the spirituals!

Reclaiming the Spirituals
Whalum challenged us to reclaim and preserve the spiritual as congregational music in the black church, and that challenge is still unmet. As he suggested (see the Appendix), our church music in the black experience is "out of line." It is out of line with those things that we call African and African American and celebrate as our

heritage. We have explored black theology, experienced the civil rights movement, and adjusted to black nationalism in the 1960s. We have investigated, examined, and adopted our African heritage through the manifestation of Afrocentricity in the 1970s. We have been spiritually energized and edified by the rushing mighty winds of neo-Pentecostalism in mainline black churches in the 1980s, and we witnessed the rise of charismatic, evangelical, Word-centered, megachurch ministries in the 1990s. God has brought us from a long way, and we have forgotten, ignored, forsaken, or buried the rich spirituals of our heritage that musically echo our hopes and fears, our faith and beliefs, our struggles and victories, and God's promises to us.

Alain Locke has suggested that the religious music of the American slave—the spirituals—displays "an epic intensity and a tragic profundity of emotional experiences, for which the only historical analogy is the spiritual experience of the Jews and the only analogue, the Psalms."[10]

Let us not be found guilty of overdressing in kente cloth (made in Korea, Hong Kong, or Taiwan), celebrating our African presence and heritage in the Bible, using African names, symbols, and rituals to help define us as African Americans, justifying and fortifying Africanisms in our African American music and worship, and yet labeling our spirituals irrelevant "cornfield ditties" or slave songs, lest we provoke God to return us to a period of enslavement. As we sing the beautiful contemporary songs of praise and worship—and we should—let us not neglect the music of yesterday that saved us, sustained us, and never left us. As the praise and worship phenomenon continues to flourish and grow, let's learn and include the indigenous, homegrown music of the African American religious experience—the spiritual—for the living of these days.

CHAPTER TEN

THE AFRICAN AMERICAN CHRISTIAN YEAR

There is an appointed time for everything.
And there is a time for every event under the heaven—
(Ecclesiastes 3:1, NASB)

T IME IS IMPORTANT! CHRISTIANITY TAKES TIME SERIOUSLY.
History is where God is made known. Christians have no
knowledge of God without time, for through events happening in historical time, God is revealed.[1] God makes his
divine nature, acts, and will known through events that
take place within the same calendar that guides and organizes the
lives of human beings.

The Christian Year and the Lectionary

Robert E. Webber says, "Christians celebrate the saving events of
God in Jesus Christ by celebrating those particular events in which
God's saving purposes were made known." The foundation of the
Christian calendar is what the New Testament calls "the Lord's
Day" (Revelation 1:10, NIV), the first day of each week. The New
Testament points to the first day of the week as a special time for
worship. Sunday stood out above all other days as the weekly
anniversary of the resurrection, or as the late Wendell P. Whalum
called them, "little Easters." In the early church, Sunday also commemorated the Lord's passion and death, but it was above all else
the day on which the Savior rose from the dead.[2]

Even the ordinary day became for the early church a structure
of praise. As the week and the day witnessed to Jesus Christ, so the

Christian Year, also called the liturgical year or the church year, became a structure for commemorating the Lord.[3] In a sermon preached in 386 John Chrysostom effectively summed up the liturgical or Christian Year: "For if Christ had not been born into the flesh he would not have been baptized, which is the Theophany [Epiphany], he would not have been crucified [some texts add: and risen], which is the Pascha [Easter], he would not have sent down the Spirit, which is the Pentecost."[4]

During the fourth century, the three great primitive feasts—Epiphany, Pascha, and Pentecost—had split from the related days—Christmas, Good Friday, and Ascension, plus some lesser days.[5] The fourth century marked the major development in the church's dramatic celebrations that expressed the central events: the manifestation, the resurrection, and the indwelling Spirit.

By the end of the fourth century the Christian Year, especially the temporal cycle, or the Easter and Christmas cycles, was fixed. Two additional celebrations were added after the fourth century: Trinity Sunday and All Saints. Trinity Sunday, the Sunday after Pentecost, represents a theological doctrine unrelated to a historical event in the life of Christ. All Saints, designated November 1 during the ninth century, commemorates the whole company of saints.

Closely related to the Christian Year is the lectionary. James White says, "If the calendar is the foundation of Christian worship, the first floor is certainly the lectionary or list of lections (scripture lessons) based on the Christian year."[6] A lectionary is a collection of readings or selections from the Scriptures, arranged and intended for proclamation during the worship of the people of God.[7]

The Revised Common Lectionary explains that "lectionaries (table of readings) were known and used in the fourth century, where major churches arranged Scripture readings according to a schedule that follows the church's year. Early lectionaries usually involved continuous reading, with each Sunday's text picking up where they left off on the previous Sunday. This practice of assigning particular readings to each Sunday and festival has continued down through the history of the Christian Church. A constant pattern, however, seems to be that the later additions of special days and feasts tended to obscure the simplicity of the original Sunday texts, so that after every few centuries, the calendar needed to be simplified and pruned in order to manifest its earlier clarity."[8]

How the Lectionary Functions

The most important function of the lectionary is to show the relationship of the readings of one Sunday to those that come before and after it. Within each of the major seasons of Advent, Christmas/Epiphany, Lent, and Easter, the flow of the season is reflected in the Scripture texts, taken together as a set for each Sunday.

The lectionary for Sundays and major festivals is arranged in a three-year cycle. The years, taken from the Synoptic Gospels, are known as Year A, the year of Matthew, Year B, the year of Mark, and Year C, the year of Luke. The first Sunday of Advent 2001, December 2, begins a new cycle of readings, which are selected from Year A, the year of Matthew, and continue through the final Sunday of the Christian Year. Then a new year begins in Advent 2002, December 1, Year B, the year of Mark. Year C, the year of Luke, begins Advent 2003, November 30, and the cycle begins again in Advent 2004, November 28.

Each Sunday the lectionary includes an Old Testament, or Hebrew Bible, reading; a psalm; a New Testament, or an Epistle, reading; and a reading from the appropriate Synoptic Gospel (Matthew, Mark, or Luke).

How the Christian Year Is Arranged

The major seasons and events of the Christian Year are organized around Advent, Christmas, Epiphany, Lent, Holy Week, Easter, and Pentecost. Let us examine each for clarity.

Advent is a fixed, penitential season of four weeks marking preparation for the coming of Christ. This coming is marked in a double manner, first in his incarnation as the Babe of Bethlehem and then in his second coming at the end of time. The season also includes a commemoration of the ministry of John the Baptist as Christ's forerunner.[9]

Christmas is a fixed season of twelve days between Christmas Day on December 25 and the beginning of Epiphany on January 6. This season focuses on the birth and infancy of Jesus Christ.

Epiphany is a season of varying length that begins January 6 and continues until Ash Wednesday, or the beginning of Lent. Its fundamental concern is the epiphany, or manifestation, of God to the world in Jesus Christ. In addition to continuing the focus on the birth of Christ, Epiphany includes the themes of the coming of the Magi to see Christ, the baptism of Jesus, Christ's visit to the temple, and the miracle of turning water into wine at the wedding in Cana of Galilee.

Lent, beginning with Ash Wednesday, is a six-week period of spiritual discipline and devotional preparation before Easter. The early church emphasized Lent as a season of instruction for baptismal candidates and as a time of fasting. The season of fasting, symbolizing Christ's forty days in the wilderness, includes the forty days before Easter (excluding Sundays). Lectionary passages tell of the ministry of Christ, his transfiguration, and the temptations.

Holy Week concludes Lent with Palm Sunday, the triumphal entry of Christ into Jerusalem; Maundy Thursday, a communion service in remembrance of the Last Supper; and Good Friday, focusing on the cross and crucifixion of Christ.

Easter, the Christian Passover or the transformation of the Jewish Passover, focuses on the resurrection of Jesus Christ. The season of Eastertide continues for fifty days, until Pentecost, and includes the ascension and reign of Christ.

Pentecost, the fiftieth day after Easter, celebrates the descent of the Holy Spirit upon the disciples and the birthday of the church as the New Israel of God.

How the Civil Year Is Arranged

In the United States we live by two approaches to time: the civil year and the academic year. The civil year begins with New Year's Day and Martin Luther King Jr. Day in January; President's Day in February; Mother's Day and Memorial Day in May; Father's Day in June; Independence Day on the fourth of July; Labor Day in

September; and Thanksgiving Day in November. The academic year begins in either August or September, with winter break in December, spring break in either March or April, and graduation in May or June. July and August are either vacation months or summer-school months.

Many Christians organize their spiritual time around the civil and academic calendars and fail to realize that they are attempting to practice their spirituality in a secular framework of time. It is even more interesting to note that while most Christians support the separation of church and state, many of the themes and occasions for worship are derived from the civil, or secular, calendar.

Most American Protestants strongly emphasized the Lord's Day, but until the twentieth century their observances of the Christian Year were largely limited to Easter and Christmas. Even Christmas was not observed in most American Protestant churches until the nineteenth century.[10]

The Calendar in African American Churches

The influence of the Christian Year and the lectionary in the African American church has been at best sporadic and in most instances nonexistent. The African Methodist Episcopal Church has traditionally followed the liturgical practices of the Methodist Episcopal church from which it was founded.

However, Baptists and Pentecostals usually have not followed the Christian Year. C. Michael Hawn asserts that two issues—avoidance of Catholic appearances and the anthropocentric emphasis upon salvation—continue to dominate the Southern Baptists' approach to the use of the Christian calendar.[11] Early English Baptist worship leaders scrupulously avoided any of trappings of the Catholic or Anglican traditions. This contrast included everything from the physical aspects of worship (e.g., use of vestments, placement of liturgical furniture and other worship aids) to the content of worship (e.g., the role of the sermon, choice of hymns or psalms sung, use of Scripture, and approach to prayer). In the minds of the early Baptists, observance of the Christian Year was linked to the worship of saints and what was called the "popish" pageantry and excess of the Roman Catholic Church. Therefore the Christian Year as an organizational scheme for the annual cycle of worship was for the most part to be avoided. Hawn continues, "The Baptist experience in America has often been directed toward the conversion of the unsaved (anthropocentric) rather than the worship of God (theocentric)."[12] The conversion emphasis was especially strong in the Sandy Creek, or revival, tradition. Even those Baptist churches whose worship reflected the more theocentric Charleston tradition usually gave little attention to the Christian Year except for the celebration of Christmas and Easter.[13]

Unless pastors have been exposed to the Christian Year through their theological education or in the church in which they grew up, most African American Baptist churches will not use the Christian Year. The traditional order of worship and events in the life of the congregation form the basis of these churches' annual calendar. The African American Christian Year is influenced and dictated by highly intricate traditions, customs, visitations, fellowships, and nonliturgical observances. These designated Sundays range from various organizations' special days, colleges' and seminaries' days, revivals, and out-of-town visitations and fellowships to home and foreign missions programs during which the church might inform and educate the congregation concerning the ministry of their program, and, in most cases, raise additional funds.

The following is a typical list of events in most African American churches that make up an annual calendar:

Pastor's Anniversary
Church Anniversary
Pastor's Aide Society Anniversary
Men's Day
Women's Day
Youth Day
Usher Boards' Anniversary
Deacons and Deaconess Sunday
Stewards Sunday
Choirs' Anniversary

NAACP Sunday
Christian Singles Sunday
Married Couples Sunday
Divorcees Sunday
Ladies Aid Sunday
Nurses Guild Sunday
Missionary Society's Anniversary
Scholarship Sunday
Stewardship Sunday
Birth-month Clubs' Sunday (January–December)
All States Club Sunday (Alabama–Wyoming)
Homecoming Sunday
African Relief Sunday
Annual Bazaar Sunday
Black History Sunday/Month
Courtesy Guild's Anniversary
Family Day
Mothers' Board Sunday
Busy Bee Circles' Anniversary
Willing Workers' Anniversary
Helping Hands Sunday
Annual Spring/Fall Tea
Revival Sunday (winter/spring/summer/fall)
Trustees' Sunday
Mother's Day
Father's Day
Martin Luther King Jr. Sunday
Founders' Sunday

In a lecture entitled "The Christian Year versus Our Year," I asked ministers how many of them observe Advent, Epiphany, Lent, and/or Pentecost as opposed to the previous list of events. The response was overwhelmingly negative. Many of them had not heard of these seasons, or if they had, they did not know what they were and thought they were Catholic, Anglican, or Euro-American Christians' observances.

In my *Directions for Music and Worship in the Twenty-first Century African American Church* (forthcoming), I asked twenty-one people—pastors, musicians, theologians, authors, and presidents of divinity school—whether or not the Christian Year and the lectionary should be used in the African American church. All of them agreed that the Christian Year and the lectionary should be used, but they immediately suggested that it be made more relevant and meaningful to African Americans and that it should include our rich sacred heritage and traditions. They also felt that hymns, spirituals, and gospels by our composers should be incorporated in the planning and that Scriptures should speak to the conditions and experiences of African Americans in language that is relevant and comprehensible to congregations. They further suggested that the King James Version (1611) of the Bible should be supplemented with the New International Version, the Revised Standard Version, and other translations for clarity.

Celebrating the African American Christian Year
"In Black . . . worship," James H. Cone says, "God is known as the Liberator of the poor and the downtrodden. God is the Almighty Sovereign One who is called a heartfixer and a mind regulator. During the worship service, God is known by the immediate presence of the divine Spirit with the people, giving them not only the vision that the society *must be transformed* but also the *power and the courage* to participate in its transformation."[14]

Liturgies and Hymnals
Trumpet in Zion by Linda H. Hollies is a new creation that seeks to address God in the voice, language, and expression of African Americans at worship. This new resource includes a call to worship, call to confession, prayer of confession, words of assurance, responsive reading based on the Psalter, offertory invitation and praise, benediction and blessing for each Sunday of the year. Scriptures are taken from the *Revised Common Lectionary*, Year A. At points information is offered about the decoration of the altar around certain themes. Hollies says that "as a pastor-teacher and faithful

student of the living Word, [she has delighted in] looking at the Old, Old Story through [her] Afri-Centric, Womanist eyes." *Trumpet in Zion* is a ready-to-use handbook for pastors and worship teams. It is offered to Christian educators for use in church school, confirmation, and small-group studies. Hollies has also completed this resource for Years B and C, and these are now published by Pilgrim Press.

African American Special Days by Cheryl Kirk-Duggan is another wonderful resource to enhance black church programming that reflects the faith-seeking, life-affirming, and freedom-longing people that we are. Each special day provides the occasion, welcome, prayer, litany, vow of commitment, suggested colors and Scriptures, and poem of reflection. It includes children and youth days, graduation and promotion days, homecoming and family reunions, Mother's Day, Father's Day, pastor's appreciation day, officers' rededication day, board and auxiliary day, choir anniversary day, and others.

The layout of each worship service is based on Scripture and African American life experience and history. The selected Scriptures embrace a psalm, an Old Testament reading, a Gospel, and an Epistle, with a focus on love, service or worship, or commitment or trust, as well as God's gift to us.

Sankofa by Grenae D. Dudley and Carlyle Fielding Stewart III is a compilation of African-based celebrations intended for use in the African American church. These celebrations include the naming of child ceremony, baptism ceremony, youth confirmation ceremony, rites of passage, the wedding ceremony, renewal of wedding vows ceremony, ritual for house blessing (*Nyumba*), a celebration of elders ceremony, a Kwanzaa service, and a celebration of the Emancipation Proclamation and a salute to black heroes. Its purpose is to help black congregations relocated themselves within the framework of African spiritual consciousness and culture and to provide a blueprint for various African-based ritual ceremonies. These rituals not only historically reconnect us with important remnants of our African past but also ground us within the cultural traditions fostered by African American spiritual praxis.[15]

The African American Heritage Hymnal, recently published by
G.I.A. Publications, Inc., contains 580 hymns (spirituals, gospel--
traditional and contemporary, praise and worship songs), 52 litanies
for the black liturgical year, and 52 responsive readings. In addition
to the great and broad body of musical selections, there is also the
feature of the Black Church Year, which provides an outline for "52
Sundays of Worshipful Celebration" with companion responsive
readings. Special celebratory litanies such as Mother's Day and
Family Day, Martin Luther King Jr. Sunday, and Grandparents'
and Elders' Day, are given. These worship tools greatly enhance the
usefulness of the *African American Heritage Hymnal* for churches of
any denomination.

Come Sunday by William B. McClain, a companion to *Songs of
Zion* published by the Section on Worship of the Board of
Discipleship of the United Methodist Church, is a worship
resource, textbook, study book, history book, and resource in black
religion. It contains chapters on "The Black Church and the Lord's
Day," "The Liturgy of Zion and the Lectionary," "Black Worship
and Black Theology," "Negro Spirituals and the Old Testament,"
and many others. In addition to offering assistance and explanations
about the contents of *Songs of Zion*, it is a scholarly yet practical
resource for pastors, musicians, and worship leaders.

In addition to the major observances of the Christian Year and
the saving events of Jesus Christ, the African American Christian
Year should include Dr. Martin Luther King Jr. Sunday; Black
History Month, with specific emphasis on Frederick Douglass,
Harriet Tubman, Booker T. Washington, Malcolm X, and others;
and Juneteenth and the Emancipation Proclamation.

As Dudley and Stewart remind us, "the African American
church has always been a vital cultural center in African American
communities. It is here that the symbols and ritual dramas of black
life are actualized, cultivated, and ceremonialized. It is within the
veil of the black church that African Americans have created, interpreted, articulated, and preserved the cultural and spiritual traditions
of both African American people and their African ancestors."
Further,

The recent rise of the Afrocentric movement, inspired in part by Ron Karenga, Molefi Asante, and others, has ignited a fervent coalescence of the cultural remnants of Africa with those of African American traditions. We are indebted to such scholars and practitioners for urging us to unapologetically reclaim those ritual and practices, which are essential to the long-term survival and sanity of African Americans as a people in America.

Accordingly, we believe that the black church must continue to be a cultural and spiritual center, calling us back to the central claims of our faith. This occurs through inculcation of the values, beliefs, and practices, which encourage cultural and spiritual creativity, and further empowers people to realize their greater human potential, both as individuals and as a community.[16]

The possibilities are endless! I have conducted several workshops, concerts, and fifth-Sunday worship services at the Trinity Baptist Church in Bronx, New York, over the past six years or more, and the pastor at Trinity Church, the Reverend Nathaniel Tyler-Lloyd, is known for his unique ability to lead worship. Every Sunday the lectionary Scriptures of the day are printed in the bulletin. During the Scripture reading, a minister may be assigned the Old Testament, or Hebrew lesson; the choir will read the psalm in unison or responsively; a layperson or another minister will read the Epistle; and the Gospel lesson may be read in unison or responsively before the sermon with the congregation standing. Every Sunday there is anticipation for the reading of the Scriptures. No two Sundays are the same. From the African American sacred music tradition, a spiritual or gospel may be inserted after the reading of one of the lessons to make its content more relevant.

Two great examples from my worship experience at the Trinity Church are offered for blending the Afrocentric with the Christocentric. On Palm Sunday, the pastor, ministers, deacons, deaconesses, and choir have processed on the powerful selection *Hosanna! Hosanna!* by Glenn Burleigh from his Easter cantata, *Let God Arise!* All the members of the procession waved palm branches. After the reading of the Epistle, the spiritual "How Did You Feel When You Come Out de Wilderness" was sung, and after the Gospel lesson, "Ride On, King Jesus." Immediately following the 7:00 A.M. service, "Jesus" was paraded around the immediate community on a rented donkey with Sunday school children following, shouting "Hosanna!"

One Pentecost Sunday, the service began with the sound of a brass ensemble, drums, tambourines, the Hammond organ and piano, and a New Orleans-style procession with red liturgical banners that entered the church. The pastor, ministers, deacons, and choir wore African attire and sang, "Lord, Let Your Holy Ghost Come On Down." The altar was covered with red, and the Scriptures for the day were punctuated with the singing of appropriate spirituals and gospels.

Devotional Writings and Sermons

The sacred writings of Howard Thurman, Zora Neale Hurston, Martin Luther King Jr., Benjamin E. Mays, Delores Williams, James Weldon Johnson, Sojourner Truth, Harriet Tubman, Frederick Douglass, Mary McCleod Bethune, Fannie Low Hamer, Bishop Desmond Tutu, Maya Angelou, Iyanla Vanzant, Samuel DeWitt Procter, Gardner C. Taylor, and countless others should be incorporated in worship in the form of responsive readings and litanies. These masterpieces should not be used during Black History month and then placed back on the shelves. *We are black all year long*, and we need substance and inspiration from our heroes and God-inspired authors and preachers all year.

Conversations with God, compiled and edited by the late James Melvin Washington, is a must for African American worship leaders, pastors, and musicians. This major contribution to African American literature is a stirring collection of more than 190 prayers that span 235 years and portray the spectrum of human emotions. These prayers should be included in our regular worship services as a connection and link to the rich legacies and heritage—suffering, hopes, joys, fears—of African American Christians.

Nor must we forget the sermons and sacred writings of Richard

Allen, Daniel Payne, and Jarena Lee with the African Methodist Episcopals. Among the African Methodist Episcopal Zions are Absalom Jones, James Varick, and Christopher Rush. Isaac Lane and Lucius Holey are representative of the Christian Methodist Episcopals, as are Nathaniel Paul, Elias C. Morris, and T. Clarkson with the African American Baptists. Then there is Charles Albert Tindley, pastor and father of African American hymnody with the United Methodists. We can read the works of William J. Seymour and C. P. Jones with the Pentecostal Holiness movement and Charles H. Mason with the Church of God in Christ. Augustus Tolton, the first African American priest, and the early members of the African American Catholic Congress cannot and must not be forgotten. Their works and words edify, encourage, challenge, and bring healing to our churches.

"The healing catharsis inherent in the Black worship service has enabled many generations of Blacks to keep their balance and sanity in a world where other racial groups with far fewer problems have chosen suicide," Henry H. Mitchell reminds us. "Statistically speaking, suicide was until recently a disease of the American white man. The Black person may have had a balm in life [that the] white man didn't know. He had a religion and a religious tradition [that] gave him a motive for being and the freedom to live. No matter what the externals of his existence, in his church he was safe in the context of love: God's love and the love of his people. It is a blessed Black tradition. The Black congregation is one of the most dynamic and healing experiences known to man. . . . The Black congregation with its contagious response . . . is the best place in the world to heal and be healed."[17]

Our rich African American heritage is vital, and preserve it we must. But let us also embrace the historical Christian heritage that has been so well preserved, organized, and structured in the Christian Year and in the lectionary. The Afrocentric must be coupled with the Christocentric as we sing a new song and perfect a more excellence praise to our God as Mt. Zion rejoices!

POSTLUDE

A S AN ORGANIST, I UNDERSTAND THE PURPOSE AND function of the postlude at the end of a worship service to be a musical "exclamation point," one which accompanies the worshipers from the security of the sanctuary back out into the world to serve God and to face new challenges with confidence, renewed faith, and assurance that God is by their side. Diane Bish once said that her favorite postludes, and the favorites of the people who stayed to listen, were those that showed the full and varied resources of the organ, not those on full organ with blasting horizontal trumpets that scared the people to death after a quiet benediction.

The Widor "Toccata" from Symphony no. 5, Vierne's "Finale" from Symphony no. 1, Mulet's "Thou Art the Rock," J. S. Bach's "Prelude and Fugue in E-flat Major," BWV 552, and Alain's "Litanies" are just five of my favorite compositions for postludes— but while certainly being crowd pleasers as well, they are not always appropriate for the church season, occasion, or mood of a given service. However, one of the most creative and inspiring postludes that I ever heard was an extremely tasteful and creative improvisation on the themes of the hymns, anthem, spiritual, and Gospel selection of that morning's worship service; it was played by my first organ teacher, the late Dr. Wendell P. Whalum, at the historic Ebenezer Baptist Church in Atlanta.

I have chosen that improvisation by Dr. Whalum as a model for this so-called postlude. It will contain themes and fragments of pre-viously discussed chapters with some further developments and embellishments. The contents of this postlude may not all be crowd pleasing, but as a whole, this culminating piece is meant to enhance, inspire, challenge, and uplift the reader as we continue to grow and develop music and worship in the African American church.

Mimicking the Megachurch: Copycats and Charismania

Many of our churches today are aggressively impersonating and attempting to reproduce the music and worship of other churches, denominations, television evangelists, and megachurch ministries without considering the community of worshipers to whom they are ministering. I have seen church choirs buy robes that are identical to other church choirs'; churches that build sanctuaries to the exact specifications of their idol's building; and churches that purchase furniture, fixtures, carpet, fabrics, and draperies to duplicate their idol's facility. Many churches implement organizational structures and titles to replicate their models. Models are certainly good if they enhance, elevate, and augment the ministry and culture of a particular congregation, but there are churches that have totally redesigned their worship and music programs to imitate others— thinking that the grass is greener on the other side—only to discover that the coveted greenery is Astroturf! The only thing missing in many of these churches are the copycat sermons to go along with their copycat buildings, organization, worship style, and appearance. Of course, with the lucrative audiotape ministries that thrive today, pastors can even plagiarize the preaching style and sermon content that they so admire.

So many of our pastors, musical directors, and worship leaders are being swept away, caught up, and awe struck by the megachurch ministries. Many of these church leaders turn to the Willow Creek, Saddleback, and World Harvest Ministries (to name a few) as the last and final word on worship and successful church growth and development. The truth is that we have in our African American churches some highly successful ministries that offer tremendous models for music ministry and church growth. These churches can and do serve as excellent models, consultants, and relevant oases for leadership development, support, and direction.

The addiction to and practice of "charismania" is alive and well in many of our churches. I define *charismania* as "the conscious misuse, impersonation, imitation, and reproduction of truly anointed, Holy-Ghost-filled worship by regimented handclapping (or applause), standing, stomping, touching your neighbors, high-fives, hollers, yells, and physical gestures," all of which "have a form of godliness but denying the power thereof" (2 Timothy 3:5). In that third chapter of 2 Timothy, Paul foretells the wickedness of the last days and describes the enemies and opponents of the truth. Titus 1:16 supports this observation when it says, "They claim to know God; but by their actions they deny him. They are detestable, disobedient, and unfit for doing anything good" (NIV).

In churches that lack strong pastoral and musical leadership, worship leaders will allow the media and music industry to set the standard and define what is good, proper, and acceptable for music and worship in that congregation. The top-forty charts and local radio station's listener hits become the guiding and sustaining authority by which musicians select music for the choir and for worship. The Broadway-Hollywood style worship that characterizes much of what we see on television has rapidly influenced mainline and traditional churches' music and worship and how it is valued. For some folks, the trip to the weekly religious theater is what keeps them going as long as it is a good show. However, if a better "religious production" opens across town or down the street, they will be there next. Whether the music is biblically based or theologically sound is not the priority of the commercialized industries that produce it. "Does it sell?" is the key question for them!

Our One Foundation: Christ-Centered Worship

Worship that is not Christ-centered becomes self-centered and egomaniacal, and should be avoided. Tragically, the "lights! cameras! action!" approach to worship reduces many worshipers who are seeking an authentic encounter with Christ to mere spectators at a rocking-n-rolling, cranked-up, good-time drama. The question before the church is an uncomfortable one: "What does the worshiper do after the benediction has been pronounced and the final doxology is sung?"

The African American church must seek sound biblical and theological foundations for its understanding and practice of worship. When we have restructured our worship on those foundations, much of what we are now experiencing will be not be tolerated and will soon fade away. Many specific elements of worship are mentioned in Scripture, such as handclapping (Psalms 47:1; 97:8), raised hands (Psalms 63:4; 134:2; 1 Timothy 2:8), choral singing and instrumental music (Exodus 15; 1 Chronicles 25:1-31; Psalm 150), congregational responses (Deuteronomy 27:15; Psalms 118:2-4; 136; 1 Corinthians 14:16), dance (Exodus 15:20; Psalms 149:3; 150:4; Jeremiah 31:4), and the choosing of leaders (Acts 1:12-26). In today's church, commands by the worship leaders to stand up, touch your neighbor, stomp the devil under your feet, jump up and down, clap your hands, run in place, dance with your partner, and so on, are quite often seen as activities by which the congregation will become more involved in worship. Unfortunately, going through these physical motions does not guarantee the spiritual involvement of the congregation—and it is the spiritual involvement that should be our priority. In the broadest sense, we must "Do it all for the glory of God" (1 Corinthians 10:31) and "for the strengthening of the church" (1 Corinthians 14:26).

Decorum and etiquette in worship must be revived, sustained, and maintained! In many cases, excessive walking, talking, chewing gum, passing notes, pagers and cell phones going off, late entrances by ministers and musicians (to name a few of the common distractions) totally divert, bewilder, disconcert, and disturb worshipers and unhinge the worship service week after week, month after month, and year after year. Constant interruptions of announcements, acknowledgments, and remarks during the service create commotion, disturbance, and diversion. There are churches whose announcement period extends longer than the sermon, and occasionally it is more memorable and enlightening! We must find strategic places in our services, either at the beginning or at the end, to deal with the concerns of the church without overwhelming the congregation with these non-worshipful items. Too often things just stay the same in hopes that they will either change or die. That is neither healthy nor realistic for the church. It has been said of cancer that early detection can, in some cases, lead to its cure. If Mt. Zion is to rejoice fully and truly, the church must be willing to adequately, honestly, and consistently evaluate its worship and non-worship—and to do so before the malignancies metastasize.

I have mentioned the urgent need to reduce the number of choirs in most churches. I have acknowledged the fact that many churches have two and three worship services each Sunday and that the need for various choirs is understandable. However, the problem in most cases is not the number of services, but the numbers of competent musicians needed to train, direct, and accompany these groups, not to mention the well-balanced voice required to sing in them. The need to recruit male voices to the church choir is understated! Most choirs that I have heard and conducted lack sufficient tenors and basses, and of course, in most gospel choirs, basses are eliminated altogether. Musicians must actively recruit men to the choir and not only men, but women as well if the alto or soprano sections are weak. Just remember, the persons recruited need to be *singers*!

Churches that have six to eight choirs generally are not able to provide or adequately compensate musical leadership for all of those choirs. In most cases, some directors are overcompensated and others are undercompensated. If the twenty-first-century African American church choir will embrace the mandate of Colossians 3:16 and sing *all* of the music of our heritage and tradition, the church can become more well rounded and enlightened. I truly believe that, and there are some wonderful examples to affirm my belief. However, achieving that goal requires competent musical leadership. We don't need quantity but *quality*.

Choosing Quality over Quantity
It is imperative that churches adequately define and identify the components and needs for music ministry in their churches. Too often churches impose styles, repertoire, and practices that are not

relevant, meaningful, or understood by the congregation. In many cases leaders are not able or not willing to equip the church with what is needed for effective music ministry. Some churches seek full-time ministers of music or directors of music, but are able to provide neither adequate space nor facilities to develop the music ministry. No program or ministry can properly grow and develop without adequate fiscal and physical resources.

I have mentioned the importance of budget. Many churches confuse musicians' salaries with a music budget. Ideally, the musicians' salary lines should be included with the ministerial staff salaries, and the music program should be a separate line item in the church budget. Churches must not become guilty of considering the choir a service department for the church, in the way that many schools, colleges, and universities consider their bands and choirs. The budget should encompass those things that are necessary to produce, maintain, and perpetuate musical excellence, items such as robes, sheet music, demo recordings, instruments, instrument maintenance, and training. (See chapter 3, pages 19–20.)

It is essential that churches develop strong instrumental programs. Not everyone sings! Many churches are organizing instrumental ensembles of strings, brass, and woodwinds. Some churches now have small to medium-sized orchestras that not only accompany the choir, but also provide accompaniment for the congregational hymns, praise and worship periods, as well as ministering instrumental preludes, offertories, and special voluntaries. It is exciting and invigorating to have brass players accompany the morning hymn or anthem in the worship. String quartets have been used most effectively during periods of meditation and reflection. While instrumental music may not be the expertise of the primary minister of music, part of that person's role is the task of finding trained leaders who *are* qualified in this facet of worship. Churches have members sitting in the pews who are wonderful musicians or who played an instrument in high school or college, and who would love to be involved in the music and worship of the church. Many band directors and orchestra leaders would welcome an opportunity to serve the church and their students.

The church leadership (e.g., pastor, deacons, stewards, trustees, etc.) must not allow the congregation to be held hostage to the limitations, arrogance, mediocrity, or lack of commitment in their musical leadership. Music ministers and musicians should be evaluated annually, biannually, or even quarterly, and these evaluations should be documented in writing and become a part of the personnel file of that staff member. Address any weaknesses identified in the evaluation with a plan of action and a timetable developed to insure implementation and improvement. Likewise, acknowledge where the evaluation identifies strengths and areas that show evidence of growth and productivity, and commend and reward the worship leader appropriately.

Develop a strategic plan for the church music ministry, and establish methods of evaluation that are realistic for a particular church. Churches must set goals and objectives, and then, most importantly, evaluate those goals. Too often, lazy pastors, officers, and administrators collect from literature published by other churches and denominations facts and information that are neither relevant nor applicable to their own church and impose external standards and criteria on their own programs. While outside data can be extremely helpful and offer direction to a church and its leadership, leaders must at all times consider the specific congregation that they are serving. Be careful not to use unrealistic measurements and standards by which to evaluate one's own ministry. Do not set goals and objectives too high *or* too low. When the expectations are too low, a church will not grow. If the expectations are unrealistically high, the church will become frustrated and perhaps even discouraged.

Finding Qualified Leadership

One of the most critical issues that must be addressed is the church musician. Too often, churches become anxious and desperate and rush to hire musicians before doing any homework on them. A church will agree to pay the musician X number of dollars for a few services to be rendered, but that all changes two or three months later. It is essential that churches establish guidelines and criteria by which they will seek applicants for positions in the music ministry. I have mentioned the importance of contractual agreements that meet the approval of both the church and the musician. Everything should be spelled out. Some folks feel that the church should not have to be concerned with such legal details. Perhaps that was the case years ago, but as we seek to more effectively and efficiently serve God in the twenty-first century, such attention to legalities *is* necessary. I have heard pastors say that they do not have contracts with their congregations. The truth of the matter is that they really should!

Be prepared with all of the following as you draft your position posting and prepare to interview candidates: the position title; the date the position is available; expected application materials (e.g., curriculum vitae, demo tapes or videos, letters of reference, etc.); specific weekly service and rehearsal requirements; additional duties as required; a brief profile of the music program; a brief profile of the congregation; type of organ and additional instruments; salary range and benefits (including vacation time); the name, address, telephone and fax numbers, and e-mail address of the church; and the name and direct telephone number of the contact person at the church.

Position descriptions should be prepared along with contracts to document the responsibilities that have been agreed upon. Generally, the position description is more specific than the contract in outlining duties and expectations. The contract deals with terms of employment, financial obligations, and additional legal clauses. It often alludes to the position description for a more specific delineation of duties.

When asked "How do you attract good musicians?" Barry Liesch, author of *The New Worship: Straight Talk on Music and the Church* answered,

> First, do what you can, with what you have, where you are.
> Second, understand that one good musician attracts another.

Third, indicate your commitment to minister pastoral care to
musicians. Fourth, adequately compensate those who are
professionally equipped, and fifth, search large churches for
potential musicians.[1]

Opportunities for professional growth and development should be
included in the musician's employment contract, and the church
must be committed to making such opportunities and resources
available in order to facilitate this expectation. However, the musician also must sincerely desire to grow and expand his or her
knowledge. There are a number of outstanding professional
workshops, clinics, conferences, and conventions at the local, state,
and national levels. The Hampton University Ministers' and
Musicians' Conference, The Gospel Music Workshop of America,
Inc., the Thomas A. Dorsey Convention, the National Association
of Negro Musicians, and Jackson State University's Church
Music Workshop of America are some of the most popular and
substantive annual conferences to which African American churches send their musicians annually to strengthen repertoire and skills.
I would also highly recommend membership in denominational
organizations and in national, state, and local professional organiza-
tions—such as the American Guild of Organists, the American
Choral Directors Association, The Hymn Society in the United
States and in Canada, the Choristers Guild, the American Guild of
English Handbell Ringers, to name a few.

However, on a more ongoing basis, our historically black colleges and universities must be challenged and supported in offering
summer and evening continuing-education programs in voice,
piano, sight singing and ear training, conducting, and instrumental
music for the church. We in the African American church must
turn to *our* institutions for academic support and training for *our*
church musicians and other continuing education needs. This partnership must be forged, strengthened, nurtured, and perpetuated!
We should not and cannot expect The Julliard School, Eastman,
Michigan, Indiana, Cincinnati, New England, or Peabody
Conservatories, or any majority institution to do what we will not

do for ourselves. Our institutions should train and adequately prepare our musicians for our churches.

It is my strong conviction that any musician who leads music in the church should be able, at the very least, to read and play a four-part hymn from the hymnal. Even if a congregation does not sing hymns, it should require its musical leaders to do so and should expect them to broaden the choir and congregation's understanding and exposure to such music appropriately. I have interviewed countless numbers of musicians who could play all over the keyboard, had perfect pitch, excellent aural skills, and extraordinary gifts and talents. However, when asked to read a familiar hymn *as it is written*, the result was embarrassing, uncomfortable, and "underwhelming" to say the least. There are those who defend these deficiencies by stating, "As long as the musician can play the music and it sounds all right to us, what difference does it make?" I don't think anyone would want a doctor, lawyer, pharmacist, or airline pilot who is being paid and in charge of your situation who has learned to perform their tasks by a natural gift for observing, listening, or imitating by trial-and-error. For the church musician (minister of music, director of music, etc.), fundamental knowledge of music, worship, and biblical studies are indispensable and should be required. The church must not allow its musical and worship leaders to *lack* in these basics.

There are incalculable, boundless, and unlimited values to reading music. It opens so many possibilities for the musician, choir, and congregation. Fortunately, most of today's popular contemporary gospel, praise and worship, and inspirational music is available on sheet music. Musicians do not have to rely on their ear or tape recorders to teach music in rehearsal. It is not only annoying, time-consuming, embarrassing, and awkward to teach music to a choir from a tape, but it is an immediate indication that the musician is limited, unprepared, and certainly unrehearsed for that particular musical selection. The choir should not even be attempting the selection until it has been mastered by the musician. Choirs should not have to endure endless clicking, rewinding, and fast-forwarding in an attempt to learn music.

Unfortunately, there are more *musicians working in churches* than there are committed *church musicians*. Therefore, we find musicians who play for synagogues on Friday, the Seventh-day Adventists on Saturday, and as many Catholic and Protestant services on Sunday as possible in order to make a decent deposit at the bank on Monday. I strongly recommend that churches *reduce* the quantity of musicians and *increase* the quality of musicians. An average-size church (with a membership between 150 and 350) should employ one minister (or director) of music and, perhaps, an associate director, and an organist, pianist, percussionist, bass guitarist, or whatever musical instrumentation is available. My teacher, the late Dr. Wendell Whalum, once observed that a church boasted of having four organists, to which observation he responded, "A church needs only one competent, well-trained organist, and perhaps a substitute when necessary. But you certainly don't need to pay two—one that can play and the other to just plunk around." The never-ceasing question, "Where can we find a musician?" will need to be addressed *proactively* instead of continuing in our current situation which has us *reactively* responding.

We must identify talented young people in our churches as well as "nontraditional" students who are willing to submit to the discipline and training needed to become proficient in ministering church music. Scholarships to quality training programs must be provided in this regard. However, specific criteria must define how and where these scholarships will be paid. They should be for students who have an expressed interest and demonstrated commitment to the music of the church, who will serve the church while completing their training, and who will make a commitment to return and serve the sponsoring congregation for a minimum number of years.

The Southern Baptist Convention of Texas has an agreement with its institutions to provided scholarships for students who commit to work in their churches while they are in school and upon graduating. We must make comparable agreements with our historically black colleges and universities whose curricula adequately prepare our students for the African American church. To the churches, these institutions must give assurance that they are able and willing to prepare students for music ministry in the African American church—a ministry of diversity. Therefore, the academic curricula must be inclusive of all styles and genres of music. The curricula must not diminish and exclude the musical contributions of Africans and African Americans and be found guilty of placing its foot on Africa as it exalts Europe and its musical traditions.

Too much of any one thing is not good, especially musical styles. It is not healthy to consume only starches at every meal. Hot dogs, hamburgers, and pizza may be good occasionally, but not for breakfast, lunch, and dinner. One must have vegetables and fruits to assure a healthy and well balanced diet. Music and worship in the twenty-first century African American church should never a limited menu of an "either-or" variety that separates generations, families, and friends. It should be a rich, anointed, spirit-filled, bountiful "both-and" buffet of praise, power, and glory, forever!

Our students need to master both the works of the Western European masters and the African and African American masters. We don't need to put down Europe to elevate Africa. God created the whole world—Europe *and* Africa: Johann S. Bach *and* Glenn Burleigh; Ludwig van Beethoven *and* William Grant Still; Igor Stravinsky *and* Andrae Crouch; Leonard Bernstein *and* Quincy Jones; Fanny Crosby *and* Lucie E. Campbell; Franz Liszt *and* Richard Smallwood; Bill Gaither *and* James Cleveland; Sandy Patti *and* Yolanda Adams; The Mormon Tabernacle Choir *and* The Morgan State University Choir; Harvard and Hampton; MIT *and* Morehouse, Standford, and Shaw.

Minister and Musician: A Pastoral Partnership
Of course, until the relationship between the minister and musician is established, nurtured, fortified, enhanced, and unswerving, at best the church will experience a "wicked waste of an opportunity for

glorifying God because of the lack of a fruitful partnership between the leadership." I have dealt with this extensively in chapter 4. Ministers and musicians must learn to work together. Musicians must listen to sermons, and ministers need to listen to music. Too many musicians are absent from the sanctuary during the sermon. (It is said that some of them take a smoke break at the point of the sermon! I certainly hope that this is not the case in God's house.) Too many ministers wait "backstage" during the opening worship in order to make a grand entrance into the sanctuary just before the sermon—or the offertory appeal. No one should be exempt from worshiping God, at any time during the service.

One of the most outstanding models of the pastoral musician was Martin Luther, who declared, "Next to the Word of God, music deserves the highest praise."[2] This statement does not exist as singular testimony to Luther's propensity for hyperbole, but rather as a summation of theological and pastoral pursuits—writing, composing, and celebrating—which affirmed his belief that next to the Word of God, music is the greatest treasure of all. Opponents of the Protestant Reformers once said that Luther did more to advance his message in his hymns than in his sermons.

Another model of the pastoral musician was Charles Albert Tindley, who is considered the father of African American hymnody. He wrote many of his hymns to complement his sermons and sang them in the midst of his preaching. Tindley was very familiar with the particular congregation for which he wrote his music. He used their language and took biblical passages and restated them in common, everyday words.

We need more Luthers and Tindleys today. Pastors and musicians can learn a lot from the work of such pastor-musicians. The church needs the partnership. Pastors and musicians must become acquainted with the basic foundations of each other's field in order to communicate more effectively the needs for music and worship in the church. The ideal music director must be (1) a musician, (2) an administrator, (3) an educator, and (4) a pastor.[3] This does not mean that the musician must be *the* pastor or even an ordained member of the clergy, but that he or she must be *pastoral* in approaching the music ministry. That is, the music director should be able to teach Sunday school and Bible study if necessary, and do visitation work in caring for choir members and the worship team.[4] Musicians and pastors can learn a lot from one another if each is willing to be a partner and team player. When this relationship is well established and perpetuated, the twenty-first-century African American church can enthusiastically and authentically sing, "Let Mt. Zion rejoice!"

APPENDIX

UNDERSTANDING THE SPIRITUALS

Following is an excerpt from a lecture by the late Wendell P. Whalum about the spiritual and its use as congregational music in the church. In this lecture, delivered at the 1981 Hampton University Ministers' Conference, Dr. Whalum maintained that spirituals could be used not only for prayer meeting and devotional music but also as functional music for the Christian Year (Advent to Pentecost). He strongly urged the black church to become acquainted with and to adopt the Christian Year, with spirituals being used at appropriate seasons.

I have already indicated that you can get them [spirituals] for every season of the church year. But when we talk about them in this sense, we're talking about them as functional music. Music that is communicative. Music that is reflective of the system that produced them. When blacks sing spirituals, they are singing them from their roots. They are singing them from an inner feeling, a kind of an outward manifestation of an inner-living essence, feeling something very deeply. Blacks have not, as a rule, . . . been afraid to enjoy their music. They have not been afraid to let it relate to something in their own lives and to recognize it as a good remedy for something in someone else's life. I went over to the bookstore here yesterday, and I found out they don't have very many, so if you are going to get one, you'd better move. Hampton has reprinted *Religious Folk-Songs of the Negro* by R. Nathaniel Dett. Now I know that a lot of churches will say, we don't sing many spirituals, because we don't know many. Well, here is a book, and you can see the size of it for those of you who can move. I'm sure they have a few more over there in the bookstore, and I believe it's nine dollars. You will never get a book like this from anywhere at that price.

Dr. Dett has given us the entire book breaking down the categories. Now this is what you must do, you must be willing, and I urge you to do this. You must sing the spirituals in the style of spirituals. I'm not confusing gospel, and please don't misunderstand me. John Work, in an article that he delivered to The Hymn Society of America in 1962, says "that gospel music is the twentieth-century spiritual." The spiritual that I am referring to is the eighteenth- and nineteenth-century spiritual. If you're going to be singing it, sing it as it is set. That is, put down these honky-tonk instruments and all of these electronic devices, put down the microphones, stop rocking, and think about the seriousness of the text that those people called illiterate in slavery put together for you to deal with. Remember as you do it that the profundity of the spiritual is not immediately apparent. I've had people say to me, "Oh, there're so simple." Well, you reveal by that that you're also dumb, because if you take a spiritual verse and dig under it in your analysis, you'll discover enough material to engage your mind for a long time. It's what my students at Morehouse call "brain-girding power." . . . Something very simple, like "Balm in Gilead," Howard Thurman made clear [that] Jeremiah ends his chapter 8 with a question mark, "Is there no balm in Gilead? Is there no physician there?" The spiritual ends it with an exclamation point—"there is, there is a Balm in Gilead!"

I think I'm hinting at it. The spiritual will help us to pull our church music in the black experience back into line. It is out of line! . . . I think that the spiritual will make us enjoy our singing without being overly simple about it. It is not difficult to sing a spiritual correctly. It doesn't take a lot of planning. It takes a mind and a heart, and it moves itself.

The other thing about the spiritual, the reason I'm urging you to return to them, is that it is congregational music. You don't need a conductor standing up swinging his arms when you sing a spiritual. You simply need a leader. It won't get too fast because your foot is not going to let it go. We call that performance practices. You don't need a choir to sing a spiritual. It's congregational music. It was group music. Spirituals were traditionally brought to the group by one person. That group would listen to the person sing it, and just like we used to do in prayer meeting, and I'm sure some of you have had this experience, they take it, and they work at it, and work at it, and work it, and make it go. Well, if it didn't, they threw it out. One thing that I've been very worried about in gospel music, we have no testing ground. Almost anything anybody writes is sung by our churches. . . . You have to be sure of what you are going to sing and how you are going to address it to God. Be very careful. Now spirituals have been to the testing ground. The ones that have survived are almost always worth your singing.

The other thing I want to say about the spiritual is that it is never intended to be funny. It is never intended to be humorous. It's the serious comment of a black people on the conditions, and it is expressing a hope in the God that they serve. Now we say that hymns are "ode of praise." All of the spirituals that I know exalt God. All of them. Therefore, I urge you to sing them.

There is another source that I wanted to give you. *American Negro Songs* by John W. Work, of whom I have spoken, from Fisk [University], put out a book, a sizeable book of spirituals originally published by Crown Press. Ask your music store to order it for you. It comes in paperback, and have a copy or two around. You don't need one for every member of the choir. Spirituals were never sung that way. You sing a spiritual by having one person know it and lead it, and the congregation and choir will take it.

John Work was a magnificent source, as was Dr. Dett, of our music. John Work tried to establish for us, not only the types, but in his book, he put them in categories where you can see the "sorrow" spirituals and the "joyful" spirituals. Beyond that, you might break them down into other aspects of our music.

This excerpt was transcribed by James Abbington and has been edited for continuity. Mrs. Patti Kinchlow of New Albany, Indiana, provided the cassette recording from which this lecture was transcribed.

NOTES

Prelude

1. W. E. B. Du Bois, *The Souls of Black Folk* (New York: Fawcett, 1961), 144.
2. C. Eric Lincoln and Lawrence H. Mamiya, *The Black Church in the African American Experience* (Durham, N.C.: Duke University Press, 1990), 346.
3. Wyatt Tee Walker, *Somebody's Calling My Name* (Valley Forge, Pa.: Judson Press, 1979), 22.
4. Carlyle Fielding Stewart III, *Black Spirituality and Black Consciousness* (Trenton, N.J.: Africa World Press, 1999), 105.
5. Thomas Peter Wahl, *The Lord's Song in a Foreign Land* (Collegeville, Minn.: Liturgical Press, 1998), 46.
6. Ibid., 47.
7. Ibid., 48.
8. Andrew Billingsley, *Mighty Like a River*, with an introduction by C. Eric Lincoln (New York: Oxford University Press, 1999), xxiii.
9. Wahl, 48.

Chapter One: The Current State of Music in the African American Church

1. Robert M. Franklin, *Another Day's Journey* (Minneapolis: Fortress, 1997), 56.
2. Cheryl J. Sanders, *Saints in Exile: The Holiness-Pentecostal Experience in African American Religion and Culture* (New York: Oxford University Press, 1996), 5.
3. C. Eric Lincoln and Lawrence Mamiya, *The Black Church in the African American Experience* (Durham, N.C.: Duke University Press, 1990), 76.
4. Wyatt Tee Walker, *Somebody's Calling My Name* (Valley Forge, Pa.: Judson Press, 1979), 24.
5. The Baptist and Methodist churches, sometimes referred to as the mainline African American churches, have tended to marginalize and criticize the Holiness-Pentecostal church, or the Sanctified church, especially for its music program. However, it is worthy of note that the Church of God in Christ (COGIC) and the Pentecostal Assemblies

of the World, Inc. (PAW) produce fine trained musicians, both vocalists and instrumentalists, and are developing orchestral organizations at their national and international conventions. Their national and international music departments are organizing for musical excellence in the new millennium and are contacting colleges and universities to further complement the training of their musicians. As denominations they provide national, regional, and state training, in addition to scholarships for further study in music education programs. They continue to offer performance experiences at the national, state, and local levels.

6. Wyatt Tee Walker, in an opening address at the 1994 Hampton University Ministers' Conference, Hampton, Virginia. To my knowledge, this address has not been published.

7. Walker, *Somebody's Calling My Name*, 188-89.

8. Wendell P. Whalum, "Music in the Churches of Black Americans: A Critical Statement," *The Black Perspective in Music* 14, no. 1 (winter 1986): 16.

9. Jon F. Eiche, *The Yamaha Guide to Sound Systems for Worship* (Milwaukee, Wis.: Hal Leonard Publishing, 1990), 8.

10. Ibid.

11. Wyatt Tee Walker, "Music Is Ministry, Just As Preaching Is Ministry," *Score Magazine* (September/October 1994), 66.

Chapter Two: Musicians in the Church

1. The list is paraphrased from Wendell P. Whalum, "Music in the Churches of Black Americans: A Critical Statement," *The Black Perspective in Music* 14, no. 1 (winter 1986): 16-17. This article is the published text of an address by the same title that was delivered at the 1985 Black American Music Symposium, University of Michigan, Ann Arbor.

2. N. Lee Orr, *The Church Music Handbook for Pastors and Musicians* (Nashville: Abingdon, 1991), 95-96.

3. Ibid., 89.

4. Harold M. Best, *Music Through the Eyes of Faith* (New York: HarperCollins, 1993), 108.

5. Rory Noland, *The Heart of the Artist* (Grand Rapids, Mich.: Zondervan, 1999), 121-22.

Chapter Three: Essentials for Church Musicians

1. Wyatt Tee Walker, "Music Is Ministry, Just As Preaching Is Ministry," *Score Magazine* (September/October 1994), 66.

2. Kenneth W. Osbeck, *Devotional Warm-Ups for the Church Choir* (Grand Rapids, Mich.: Kregel, 1985), 24-25.

3. Paul Westermeyer, *Te Deum* (Minneapolis: Fortress, 1998), 1-2.

N O T E S

4. The Professional Concerns Committee of the American Guild of Organists' Detroit and Ann Arbor chapter provides this checklist of responsibilities in "The Employment of Musicians in Churches and Synagogues" (1994).
5. N. Lee Orr, *The Church Music Handbook for Pastors and Musicians* (Nashville: Abingdon, 1991), 89-94.
6. Ibid., 98.
7. C. Harry Causey, *Things They Didn't Tell Me about Being a Minister of Music* (Rockville, Md.: Music Revelation, 1988).
8. James Robert Davidson, *A Dictionary of Protestant Church Music* (Metuchen, N.J.: Scarecrow, 1975), 205-206.
9. Periodically, the American Guild of Organists (AGO) publishes a resource called "The Employment of Musicians in Churches and Synagogues," which offers valuable guidelines for the church striving to develop its own position descriptions and job responsibilities for its staff musicians.
10. Carol Doran and Thomas H. Troeger, *Trouble at the Table* (Nashville: Abingdon, 1992), 76.
11. Ibid., 76-77.
12. Ibid., 88-89.

Chapter Four: The Relationship between Pastors and Musicians
1. Eric Routley, *Church Music and Theology* (Philadelphia: Muhlenberg, 1959), 110.
2. N. Lee Orr, *The Church Music Handbook for Pastors and Musicians* (Nashville: Abingdon, 1991), 54.
3. Ibid., 55.
4. Ibid., 59-66.
5. Ibid., 67-70.
6. Carol Doran and Thomas H. Troeger, *Trouble at the Table* (Nashville: Abingdon, 1992), 79.
7. Ibid., 78-83.
8. Wyatt Tee Walker, "Music Is Ministry, Just As Preaching Is Ministry," *Score Magazine* (September/October 1994), 66.
9. James Abbington, "Directions for Music and Worship in the Twenty-first Century African American Church: Interviews with Pastors, Theologians and Musicians." Presented in partial fulfillment of the requirements for the degree Doctor of Musical Arts, Horace H. Rackham School of Graduate Studies, The University of Michigan (Ann Arbor), 1999. Unpublished.

Chapter Five: Choirs in the Church
1. J. Wendell Mapson Jr., *The Ministry of Music in the Black Church* (Valley

ᵉᵉᵉᵉᵉ
ᵉᵉ

Forge, Pa.: Judson Press, 1976), 42.

2. Floyd Massey Jr. and Samuel B. McKinney, *Church Administration in the Black Perspective* (Valley Forge, Pa.: Judson Press, 1976), 42.

3. Mapson, 75-76.

4. See Robert H. Mitchell, *I Don't Like That Music* (Carol Stream, Ill.: Hope Publishing Company, 1993).

5. Waldo S. Pratt, *Musical Ministries in the Church* (New York: G. Schirmer, 1923).

6. Austin C. Lovelace and William C. Rice, *Music and Worship in the Church* (Nashville: Abingdon, 1976), 89-90.

7. Ibid., 88.

8. Ruth Nininger, *Church Music Comes of Age* (New York: Carl Fischer, 1957), 13.

9. Joseph Ashton, *Music in Worship* (Boston: Pilgrim, 1943), 132.

10. From Mapson, 78-82.

11. Ibid., 83.

12. Calvin M. Johansson, *Discipling Music Ministry* (Peabody, Mass.: Hendrickson, 1992), 117.

13. Ibid., 117-18.

14. Ibid., 119.

15 Ibid.

Chapter Six: Planning Worship

1. William D. Watley, "Theological Linguistics," an address delivered at the 2000 Hampton University Ministers Conference, Hampton, Virginia. To my knowledge, this address has not been published.

2. John F. Wilson, *An Introduction to Church Music* (Chicago: Moody Press, 1965), 30.

3. Melva Wilson Costen, *African American Christian Worship* (Nashville: Abingdon, 1993), 77.

4. Ibid., 77-78.

5. A. W. Tozer, *Tozer on Worship and Entertainment*, comp. James L. Snyder (Camp Hill, Pa.: Christian Publications, 1997), 101-2.

6. Ibid., 111-12, 115.

7. Robert E. Webber, *Worship Is a Verb* (Peabody, Mass.: Hendrickson, 1995), 13.

8. Ibid.; see 16-18.

9. C. Welton Gaddy, *The Gift of Worship* (Nashville: Broadman, 1992), xi.

10. A. S. Herbert, *Worship in Ancient Israel* (Richmond, Va.: John Knox, 1963), 47.

11. William Temple, *Readings in St. John's Gospel* (London: Macmillan, 1940), 68, cited by John W. Carlton, "Preaching and Worship," *Review and Expositor* (summer 1965): 319.

12. Paul W. Hoon, *The Integrity of Worship* (Nashville: Abingdon, 1971), 77.

N O T E S

13. Frederick H. Talbot, *African American Worship* (Lima, Ohio: Fairway Press, 1998), 135.

14. Tozer, 114.

15. Costen; see 134-40.

16. Howard Stevenson, "Planning Worship," in *Leadership Handbook of Preaching and Worship*, ed. James D. Berkley (Grand Rapids, Mich.: Baker Books, 1992); see 171-96.

17. Ibid., 179.

18. Talbot, 77.

19. Watley.

20. Zan W. Holmes Jr., *Encountering Jesus* (Nashville: Abingdon, 1992), 38-39.

21. Ibid.; see chapter 3, "Encountering Jesus in Worship," 31-45.

Chapter Seven: Hymnody in the Church

1. C. Welton Gaddy, *The Gift of Worship* (Nashville: Broadman, 1992), 155.

2. William J. Reynolds and Milburn Price, *A Survey of Christian Hymnody* (Carol Stream, Ill.: Hope Publishing Company, 1987), v.

3. Diana Sanchez, *Your Ministry of Planning and Leading Hymn Festivals* (Nashville: Discipleship Resources, 1990), 2-3.

4. S. Paul Schilling, *The Faith We Sing* (Philadelphia: Westminster, 1983), 23.

5. Ibid.

6. J. Wendell Mapson Jr., *Strange Fire* (St. Louis, Mo.: Hodale, 1996), 85. The material was first presented as lectures at the 1995 and 1996 Hampton University Ministers' Conference, Hampton, Virginia.

7. Wyatt Tee Walker, *Somebody's Calling My Name* (Valley Forge, Pa.: Judson Press, 1979), 17.

8. Ibid., 118-19.

9. Wendell P. Whalum, "Black Hymnody," in *Black Church Lifestyles*, ed. Emmanuel L. McCall (Nashville: Broadman, 1986), 91.

10. J. Wendell Mapson Jr., *The Ministry of Music in the Black Church* (Valley Forge, Pa.: Judson Press, 1976), 18.

11. Walker, 98.

12. Schilling, 42.

13. See the preface of *The Hymn Book* of the Anglican Church of Canada and the United Church of Canada, February 1, 1971, authorized by the General Synod and General Council.

14. Schilling, 43.

15. Ibid., 44.

16. Wyatt Tee Walker, *Afrocentrism and Christian Faith* (New York: Martin Luther King Fellows Press, 1993), 13-16. With the word *eschatos-centered*, Walker refers to

the promised future of the Christian, as in such hymns as "Just to Behold His Face," "When We All Get to Heaven," "I'll Fly Away," and "The Unclouded Day."

17. Howard Stevenson, "Keys to Congregational Singing," in *Leadership Handbook of Preaching and Worship*, ed. James D. Berkley (Grand Rapids, Mich.: Baker Books, 1992), 301.

18. Robin A. Leaver, "The Theological Character of Music in Worship," in *Duty and Delight*, ed. Robin A. Leaver, James Litton, and Carlton R. Young (Carol Stream, Ill.: Hope Publishing Company, 1985), 49.

Chapter Eight: Anthems in the Church

1. Quoted in Miles Mark Fisher, *Negro Slave Songs in the United States* (Ithaca, N.Y.: Cornell University Press, 1953), 190.

2. Eileen Southern, ed., *Readings in Black American Music* (New York: Norton, 1971), 69-70.

3. The practice of lining out hymns was a holdover from eighteenth-century English musical tradition. The English practice was to have a deacon recite the hymn line before the congregation sang it. African Americans "blackened" this tradition, which came to be called "lining meter hymns," but the hymns were performed a cappella. Wyatt Walker discusses this tradition in his book, *Somebody's Calling My Name* (Valley Forge, Pa.: Judson Press, 1979).

4. Southern, 65.

5. Ibid., 66.

6. Ibid., 68.

7. Charles G. Adams, "Some Aspects of Black Worship," *Andover Newton Quarterly* 11, no. 3 (January 1971): 126.

8. William B. Garcia, "Church Music by Black Composers: A Bibliography of Choral Music," in *The Black Perspective in Music* 2, no. 2 (fall 1974): 145.

9. Evelyn Davidson White, *Choral Music by African-American Composers*, 2nd ed. (Lanham, Md.: Scarecrow, 1996).

10. Harold M. Best, *Music Through the Eyes of Faith* (New York: HarperCollins, 1993), 122-23.

11. See note 6.

12. Charles G. Adams, "Pastor's Word," printed in the program booklet for the annual We Sing Praises concert of the Jubilee Chorus, November 15, 1992, at the Hartford Memorial Baptist Church in Detroit, Michigan, 2.

13. Paul Westermeyer, *Te Deum* (Minneapolis: Fortress, 1998), 293.

14. Ibid. See also William D. Watley's *Singing the Lord's Song in a Strange Land* (Grand Rapids, Mich.: Eerdmans, 1993).

15. Wendall P. Whalum, in a lecture entitled "Music in the Black Church" delivered at the 1987 Hampton University Ministers' Conference, Hampton, Virginia.

N O T E S

To my knowledge, this address has not been published.
16. Adams, "Pastor's Word," 2.

Chapter Nine: The Spiritual as Congregational Music

1. Howard Thurman, "The Negro Spiritual Speaks of Life and Death," in *Deep River* and *The Negro Spiritual Speaks of Life and Death* (1945; c. 1955; Richmond, Ind.: Friends United Press, 1975), 38.
2. Compare ibid., Miles Mark Fisher, *Negro Slave Songs in the United States* (1953; New York: Carol Publishing, 1990), John Lovell, *Black Song* (New York: Macmillan, 1972), and Lawrence W. Levine, *Black Culture and Black Consciousness* (New York: Oxford University Press, 1977).
3. John W. Work III, *Folk Songs of the American Negro* (New York: Greenwood, 1969), 37.
4. Fisher, 176-77.
5. Lovell, 111.
6. Wendell P. Whalum, "Black Hymnody," in *Black Church Lifestyles*, ed. Emmanuel L. McCall (Nashville: Broadman, 1986), 85.
7. Zora Neale Hurston, *The Sanctified Church* (Berkeley, Calif.: Turtle Island Press, 1981), 79-81.
8. R. Nathaniel Dett, *Religious Folk-Songs of the Negro* (Hampton, Va.: Hampton Institute Press, 1927), 267.
9. Edward Boatner and Willa A. Townsend, eds., *Spirituals Triumphant* (Nashville: Sunday School Publishing Board of the National Baptist Convention, USA, Inc., 1927), foreword by A. M. Townsend.
10. Alain Locke, "The Negro Spirituals," in *Black Expressions*, ed. Addison Gayle Jr. (New York: Weybright and Talley, 1969), 48-49.

Chapter Ten: The African American Christian Year

1. Hoyt L. Hickman, Don E. Saliers, Laurence H. Stookey, and James F. White, *The New Handbook of the Christian Year* (Nashville: Abingdon, 1992), 16.
2. James F. White, *Introduction to Christian Worship* (Nashville: Abingdon, 1990), 57.
3. Ibid., 58.
4. John Chrysostom, *Opera Omnia*, ed. Bernard de Montfaucon (Paris: Daume, 1834), 2:418.
5. Hickman, Saliers, Stookey, and White, 24.
6. White, 81.
7. *The Revised Common Lectionary* (Nashville: Abingdon, 1992), 9.
8. Ibid.
9. The definitions for the various seasons of the Christian Year in this chapter

133

derive from respective articles by R. F. Burton in *The New Westminster Dictionary of Liturgy and Worship* (Philadelphia: Westminster, 1986). Readers are encouraged to consult this resource for more definition of and background about each season.

10. Hickman, Saliers, Stookey, and White, 26.

11. C. Michael Hawn, "Baptist Hymnody and the Christian Year," in *Faith and Mission 8*, no. 2 (spring 1991), 49.

12. Ibid.

13. See Walter Shurden, *Not a Silent People* (Nashville: Broadman, 1972) for a more detailed account of the Sandy Creek and Charleston traditions among early Baptists in America.

14. James H. Cone, "Sanctification and Liberation in Black Religious Tradition," in *Sanctification and Liberation*, ed. Theodore Runyon (Nashville: Abingdon, 1981), 182.

15. Carlyle Fielding Stewart III, *Soul Survivors* (Louisville, Ky.: Westminster John Knox, 1997).

16. Grenae D. Dudley and Carlyle Fielding Stewart III, *Sankofa* (Cleveland: United Church Press, 1997), x.

17. Henry H. Mitchell, *Black Preaching* (Nashville: Abingdon, 1990), 111.

Postlude

1. Barry Liesch, *The New Worship: Straight Talk on Music and the Church* (Grand Rapids, Mich.: Baker Book House, 1996), 230–32.

2. *Luther's Works*, vol. 53, *Liturgy and Hymns*, ed. Leupold (Philadelphia: Fortress Press, 1965), 323.

3. Donald P. Hustad, *Jubilate! Church Music in the Evangelical Tradition* (Carol Stream, Ill.: Hope Publishing Company, 1981), 49–50.

4. Liesch, 216.

BIBLIOGRAPHY

Aghahowa, Brenda Eatman. *Praising in Black and White: Unity and Diversity in Christian Worship*. Cleveland: United Church Press, 1996.

Anderson, Leith. *A Church for the 21st Century: Bringing Change to Your Church to Meet the Challenges of a Changing Society*. Minneapolis: Bethany House Publishers, 1992.

Bell, Derrick. *Gospel Choirs: Psalms of Survival in an Alien Land Called Home*. New York: Basic Books, 1996.

Bell, John L. *The Singing Thing: A Case for Congregational Song*. Chicago: GIA Publications, 2000.

Berkley, James D., ed. *Leadership Handbook of Preaching and Worship*. Grand Rapids: Baker Book House Company, 1992.

Best, Harold M. *Music Through the Eyes of Faith*. New York: HarperCollins Publishers, 1993.

Borsch, Frederick Houk. *Introducing the Lessons of the Church Year: A Guide for Lay Readers and Congregations*. New York: Seabury Press, 1978.

Bower, Peter C., ed. *Handbook for the Revised Common Lectionary*. Louisville: Westminster John Knox Press, 1996.

Boyer, Horace Clarence. *How Sweet the Sound: The Golden Age of Gospel*. Washington, D.C.: Elliott and Clark Publishing, 1995.

Brueggemann, Walter. *Praying the Psalms*. Winona, Minn.: Saint Mary's Press, 1982.

———. *The Message of the Psalms: A Theological Commentary*. Minneapolis: Augsburg Publishing House, 1984.

———. *The Psalms and the Life of Faith*. Ed. Patrick D. Miller. Minneapolis: Fortress Press, 1995.

Burroughs, Bob. *An ABC Primer for Church Musicians*. Nashville: Broadman Press, 1990.

Carson, Tim and Kathy. *So You're Thinking about Contemporary Worship*. St. Louis: Chalice Press, 1997.

Causey, C. Harry. *Things They Didn't Tell Me about Being a Minister of Music*. Rockville, Md.: Music Revelation, 1988.

Chapman, Mark L. *Christianity on Trial: African-American Religious Thought before and after Black Power*. Maryknoll, N.Y.: Orbis Books, 1996.

Cherwien, David M. *Let the People Sing!* St. Louis: Concordia Publishing House, 1997.

Clark, Linda J. *Music in Churches: Nourishing Your Congregation's Musical Life*. New York: An Alban Institute Publication, 1994.

Cone, James H. *The Spiritual and the Blues*. Maryknoll, N.Y.: Orbis Books, 1972.

Costen, Melva Wilson. *African American Christian Worship*. Nashville: Abingdon Press, 1993.

Davidson, James Robert. *A Dictionary of Protestant Church Music*. Metuchen, N.J.: The Scarecrow Press, 1975.

Davies, J. G., ed. *The New Westminster Dictionary of Liturgy and Worship*. Philadelphia: The Westminster Press, 1986.

Dawn, Marva J. *Reaching Out without Dumbing Down: A Theology of Worship for the Turn-of-the-Century Culture*. Grand Rapids, Mich.: William B. Eerdmans Publishing Company, 1995.

———. *A Royal "Waste" of Time: The Splendor of Worshiping God and Being Church for the World*. Grand Rapids, Mich.: William B. Eerdmans Publishing Company, 1999.

Dean, Talmage W. *A Survey of Twentieth Century Protestant Church Music in America*. Nashville: Broadman Press, 1988.

Doran, Carol, and Thomas H. Troeger. *Trouble at the Table: Gathering the Tribes for Worship*. Nashville: Abingdon Press, 1992.

Dozer, Dan. *Come Let Us Adore Him: Dealing with the Struggle over Style of Worship in Christian Churches and Churches of Christ*. Joplin, Mo.: College Press Publishing Company, 1994.

DuBois, W. E. B. *The Souls of Black Folk*. New York: Dover Publications, 1994.

Dudley, Grenae D., and Carlyle F. Stewart III. *Sanfoka: Celebrations for the African American Church*. Cleveland: United Church Press, 1997.

Dyson, Michael Eric. *Between God and Gangsta Rap: Bearing Witness to Black Culture*. New York: Oxford University Press, 1996.

Easum, William. *Dancing with Dinosaurs: Ministry in a Hostile and Hurting World*. Nashville: Abingdon Press, 1993.

Ellinwood, Leonard. *The History of American Church Music*. New York: Morehouse-Gorham Company, 1953.

Esken, Harry, and Hugh T. McElrath. *Sing with Understanding: An Introduction to Christian Hymnody*. Second edition, revised and expanded. Nashville: Church Street Press, 1995.

Evans, James H., Jr. *We Have Been Believers: An African-American Systematic Theology*. Minneapolis: Fortress, 1992.

———. *We Shall All Be Changed: Social Problems and Theological Renewal*. Minneapolis: Fortress, 1997.

Fisher, Miles Mark. *Negro Slave Songs in the United States*. New York: Citadel Press, 1953.

Floyd, Samuel A., Jr. *The Power of Black Music: Interpreting Its History from Africa to the United States*. New York: Oxford University Press, 1995.

Frame, John M. *Worship in Spirit and Truth: A Refreshing Study of the Principles and Practice of Biblical Worship*. Phillipsburg, N.J.: P & R Publishing, 1996.

Franklin, Robert M. *Another Day's Journey: Black Churches Confronting the American Crisis*. Minneapolis: Fortress Press, 1997.

Gaddy, C. Welton. *The Gift of Worship*. Nashville: Broadman Press, 1992.

Goatley, David Emmanuel. *Were You There? Godforsakenness in Slave Religion*. Maryknoll, N.Y.: Orbis Books, 1996.

Hackett, Charles D., and Don Saliers. *The Lord Be with You: A Visual Handbook for Presiding in Christian Worship.* Cleveland: OSL Publications, 1990.

Harris, Michael W. *The Rise of Gospel Blues: The Music of Thomas Andrew Dorsey in the Urban Church.* New York: Oxford University Press, 1992.

Hickman, Hoyt L., Don E. Saliers, Laurence Hull Stokey, and James White. *The New Handbook of the Christian Year.* Nashville: Abingdon Press, 1992.

Hoffman, Lawrence A., and Janet R. Walton, eds. *Sacred Sound and Social Change: Liturgical Music in Jewish and Christian Experience.* Notre Dame: University of Notre Dame Press, 1992.

Holck, Manfred, Jr., compiler. *Dedication Services for Every Occasion.* Valley Forge: Judson Press, 1984.

Hollies, Linda H. *Trumpet in Zion: Year A. Worship Resources.* Cleveland: Pilgrim Press, 2001.

Holmes, Zan W., Jr. *Encountering Jesus.* Nashville: Abingdon Press, 1992.

Hood, Robert E. *Begrimed and Black: Christian Traditions on Blacks and Blackness.* Minneapolis: Fortress Press, 1994.

———. *Must God Remain Greek? Afro Cultures and God-talk.* Minneapolis: Fortress Press, 1990.

Hoon, Paul Waitman. *The Integrity of Worship.* Nashville: Abingdon Press, 1971.

Hooper, William L. *Ministry and Musicians: The Role of Ministry in the Work of Church Musicians.* Nashville: Broadman Press, 1986.

Hunter, James Davison. *Culture Wars: The Struggle to Define America.* New York: Basic Books, 1991.

Hurston, Zora Neale. *The Sanctified Church.* Berkeley, Calif.: Turtle Island, 1981.

Hustad, Donald P. *Jubilate! Church Music in the Evangelical Tradition.* Carol Stream, Ill.: Hope Publishing Company, 1981.

———. *Jubilate II: Church Music in Worship and Renewal.* Carol Stream, Ill.: Hope Publishing Company, 1993.

Jackson, Irene V., ed. *Afro-American Religious Music: A Bibliography and Catalogue of Gospel Music.* Westport, Conn.: Greenwood Press, 1979.

Johansson, Calvin M. *Discipling Music Ministry: Twenty-first Century Directions.*

Peabody, Mass.: Hendrickson Publishers, 1992.

———. *Music and Ministry: A Biblical Counterpoint*. Second edition. Peabody, Mass.: Hendrickson Publishers, 1998.

Jones, Arthur C. *Wade in the Water: The Wisdom of the Spirituals*. Maryknoll, N.Y.: Orbis Books, 1993.

Jones, Cheslyn, Geoffrey Wainwright, Edward Yarnold, and Paul Bradshaw, eds. *The Study of Liturgy*. Revised edition. Oxford: Oxford University Press, 1992.

Jordan, James. *Evoking Sound: Fundamentals of Choral Conducting and Rehearsing*. Chicago: GIA Publications, 1996.

———. *The Musician's Soul*. Chicago: GIA Publications, 1999.

Keener, Craig S., and Glenn Usry. *Defending Black Faith: Answers to Tough Questions about African-American Christianity*. Downers Grove, Ill.: Inter-Varsity Press, 1997.

Keikert, Patrick R. *Welcoming the Stranger: A Public Theology of Worship and Evangelism*. Minneapolis: Fortress Press, 1992.

Kirk-Duggan, Cheryl A. *African American Special Days: 15 Complete Worship Services*. Nashville: Abingdon Press, 1996.

———. *Exorcizing Evil: A Womanist Perspective on the Spirituals*. Maryknoll, N.Y.: Orbis Books, 1997.

Liesch, Barry. *The New Worship: Straight Talk on Music and the Church*. Grand Rapids, Mich.: Baker Book House, 1996.

Lincoln, C. Eric, and Lawrence Mamiya. *The Black Church in the African American Experience*. Durham, N.C.: Duke University Press, 1990.

Lovelace, Austin C., and William C. Rice. *Music and Worship in the Church*. Nashville: Abingdon Press, 1976.

Lovell, John, Jr. *Black Song: The Forge and the Flame*. New York: Macmillan, 1972.

Mapson, Wendell J., Jr. *The Ministry of Music in the Black Church*. Valley Forge, Pa.: Judson Press, 1984.

———. *Strange Fire: A Study of Worship and Liturgy in the African American Church*. St. Louis, Mo.: Hodale Press, 1996.

Marshall, Madeleine Forell. *Common Hymnsense.* Chicago: GIA Publications, 1995.

McClain, William B. *Come Sunday: The Liturgy of Zion.* Nashville: Abingdon Press, 1990.

Migliore, Daniel L. *Faith Seeking Understanding: An Introduction to Christian Theology.* Grand Rapids, Mich.: William B. Eerdmans Publishing Company, 1991.

Mitchell, Robert H. *I Don't Like That Music.* Carol Stream, Ill.: Hope Publishing Company, 1993.

Myers, Kenneth A. *All God's Children and Blue Suede Shoes: Christians and Popular Culture.* Wheaton, Ill.: Crossway Books, 1989.

Niebuhr, H. Richard. *Christ and Culture.* New York: Harper and Row Publishers, 1951.

Noland, Rory. *The Heart of the Artist: A Character-Building Guide for You and Your Ministry Team.* Grand Rapids, Mich.: Zondervan Publishing House, 1999.

Orr, N. Lee. *The Church Music Handbook for Pastors and Musicians.* Nashville: Abingdon Press, 1991.

Owens, Bill. *The Magnetic Music Ministry.* Nashville: Abingdon Press, 1996.

Pass, David B. *Music and the Church: A Theology of Church Music.* Nashville: Broadman Press, 1989.

Pitts, Walter F., Jr. *Old Ship of Zion: The Afro-Baptist Ritual in the African Diaspora.* New York: Oxford University Press, 1993.

Raboteau, Albert J. *Slave Religion: The "Invisible Institution" in the Antebellum South.* New York: Oxford University Press, 1978.

Raboteau, Robert J. *A Fire in the Bones: Reflections on African-American Religious History.* Boston: Beacon Press, 1995.

Reagon, Bernice Johnson, ed. *We'll Understand It Better By and By: Pioneering African American Gospel Composers.* Washington, D.C.: Smithsonian Institution Press, 1992.

Routley, Erik. *Church Music and the Christian Faith.* Carol Stream, Ill.: Agape, 1978.

BIBLIOGRAPHY

———. *Twentieth Century Church Music.* Carol Stream, Ill.: Agape, 1964.

Saliers, Don E. *Worship as Theology: Foretaste of Glory Divine.* Nashville: Abingdon Press, 1994.

———. *Worship Come to Its Senses.* Nashville: Abingdon Press, 1996.

Sanders, Cheryl J. *Saints in Exile: The Holiness-Pentecostal Experience in African American Religion and Culture.* New York: Oxford University Press, 1996.

Schilling, S. Paul. *The Faith We Sing: How the Message of Hymns Can Enhance Christian Belief.* Philadelphia: Westminster Press, 1983.

Schultze, Quentin J., et al. *Dancing in the Dark: Youth, Popular Culture, and the Electronic Media.* Grand Rapids, Mich.: William B. Eerdmans, 1991.

Segler, Franklin M. *Understanding, Preparing for, and Practicing Christian Worship.* Second edition, revised by Randall Bradley. Nashville: Broadman and Holman Publishers, 1996.

Senn, Frank. *Christian Liturgy: Catholic and Evangelical.* Minneapolis: Fortress Press, 1997.

Southern, Eileen. *The Music of Black Americans: A History.* Third edition. New York: W. W. Norton and Company, 1997.

———. *Readings in Black American Music.* New York: W. W. Norton and Company, 1971.

Spencer, Donald A. *Hymn and Scripture Selection Guide: A Cross-Reference Tool for Worship Leaders.* Grand Rapids, Mich.: Baker Book House, 1993.

Spencer, Jon Michael. *Black Hymnody: A Hymnological History of the African-American Church.* Knoxville: The University of Tennessee Press, 1992.

———. *Protest and Praise: Sacred Music of Black Religion.* Minneapolis: Fortress Press, 1990.

———. *Sing a New Song: Liberating Black Hymnody.* Minneapolis: Fortress Press, 1995.

Stewart, Carlyle F., III. *African American Church Growth: 12 Principles for Prophetic Ministry.* Nashville: Abingdon Press, 1994.

———. *Black Spirituality and Black Consciousness: Soul Force, Culture and Freedom in the African-American Experience.* Trenton, N.J.: Africa World Press, 1999.

————. *Soul Survivors: An African American Spirituality.* Louisville: Westminster John Knox Press, 1997.

Talbot, Frederick H. *African American Worship: New Eyes for Seeing.* Lima, Ohio: Fairway Press, 1998.

The Liturgy Documents: A Parish Resource, Third edition. Chicago: Liturgy Training Publications, 1991.

The Psalms: An Inclusive Language Version Based on the Grail Translation from the Hebrew. Chicago: GIA Publications, 2000.

The Revised Common Lectionary: The Consultation on Common Texts. Nashville: Abingdon Press, 1992.

Thompson, Bard. *A Bibliography of Christian Worship.* Metuchen, N.J.: The American Theological Association and The Scarecrow Press, 1989.

Tozer, A. W. *Tozer on Worship and Entertainment.* Compiled by James L. Snyder. Camp Hill, Pa.: Christian Publications, 1997.

Vitz, Paul C. *Psychology as Religion: The Cult of Self-Worship.* Second edition. Grand Rapids, Mich.: William B. Eerdmans, 1994.

Wahl, Thomas Peter. *The Lord's Song in a Foreign Land.* Collegeville, Pa.: The Liturgical Press, 1998.

Walker, Wyatt Tee. *Somebody's Calling My Name: Black Sacred Music and Social Change.* Valley Forge, Pa.: Judson Press, 1979.

Wallace, Robin Knowles. *Things They Never Tell You before You Say "Yes": The Nonmusical Tasks of the Church Musician.* Nashville: Abingdon Press, 1994.

Warren, Gwendolin Sims. *Ev'ry Time I Feel the Spirit: 101 Best-Loved Psalms, Gospel Hymns, and Spiritual Songs of the African-American Church.* New York: Henry Holt and Company, 1997.

Washington, James Melvin. *Conversations with God: Two Centuries of Prayers by African Americans.* New York: HarperCollins Publishers, 1994.

Webber, Robert. *Planning Blended Worship: The Creative Mixture of Old and New.* Nashville: Abingdon Press. 1998.

————. *Worship Is a Verb: Eight Principles for Transforming Worship.* Second edition. Peabody, Mass.: Hendrickson Publishers, 1995.

Westermeyer, Paul. *The Church Musician.* Revised edition. Minneapolis: Augsburg Fortress, 1997.

————. *Let Justice Sing: Hymnody and Justice*. Collegeville, Pa.: The Liturgical Press, 1998.

————. *Te Deum: The Church and Music*. Minneapolis: Fortress, 1998.

————. *With Tongues of Fire: Profiles in 20th-Century Hymn Writing*. St. Louis: Concordia Publishing House, 1995.

Wilmore, Gayraud S. *Last Things First: Library of Living Faith*. Philadelphia: The Westminster Press, 1982.

Wilson-Dickson, Andrew. *The Story of Christian Music*. Minneapolis: Fortress Press, 1996.

Wimbush, Vincent L., ed. *African Americans and The Bible: Sacred Texts and Social Textures*. New York: Continuum International Publishing Group, 2000.

Wren, Brian. *Praying Twice: The Music and Words of Congregational Song*. Louisville: Westminster John Knox Press, 2000.

Wright, Jeremiah A., Jr. *Africans Who Shaped the Faith: A Study of 10 Biblical Personalities*. Chicago: Urban Ministries, 1995.

Wuthnow, Robert. *Christianity in the 21st Century: Reflections on the Challenges Ahead*. New York: Oxford University Press, 1993.

————. *Rediscovering the Sacred: Perspectives on Religion in Contemporary Society*. Grand Rapids, Mich.: William B. Eerdmans Publishing Company, 1992.